unchaᴩted teᴩᴩitoᴩies

adventures in learning

hywel ᴩobeᴩts & debᴩa kidd

illustᴩated by gabᴩiel kidd

Independent Thinking Press

First published by

Independent Thinking Press, Crown Buildings, Bancyfelin, Carmarthen, Wales, SA33 5ND, UK

www.independentthinkingpress.com

Independent Thinking Press is an imprint of Crown House Publishing Ltd.

First published 2018. Reprinted 2018.

Independent Thinking Press has no responsibility for the persistence or accuracy of URLs for external or third-party websites referred to in this publication, and does not guarantee that any content on such websites is, or will remain, accurate or appropriate.

British Library of Cataloguing-in-Publication Data

A catalogue entry for this book is available from the British Library.

Print ISBN: 978-178135295-3
Mobi ISBN: 978-178135302-8
ePub ISBN: 978-178135303-5
ePDF ISBN: 978-178135304-2

Printed and bound in the UK by
TJ International, Padstow, Cornwall

Foreword

I am delighted and honoured to have been asked to write the foreword to this book, the authors of which are colleagues with whom I have had the privilege to work on more than one occasion. Every time I have done so, I have learned a great deal and this book captures a huge amount of that learning.

It is a book that offers ideas and practical suggestions that can be translated into the classroom to the benefit of teachers and learners. It will be a treasure trove that you can return to again and again to find inspiration, strategies and tools.

It is also a book that contains arguments and ideas. It is much more than a handbook – much more, even, than a very good toolkit. I read it from cover to cover and was struck by the way in which all the elements of the book blend together to achieve the ambition that it sets for itself. It is "an unabashed call to arms for the imagination".

It encourages you to work with ideas from young people, identify their strengths, give them the chance to co-construct the learning and help them to tap into their potential. It also answers the question that I keep asking: "How do you know what the potential of learners is, unless you allow them to surprise you?" This book is full of contexts and questions which offer that opportunity.

"But what about knowledge, discipline and attainment?" you might ask. The answer is that these elements are all here too. Debra and Hywel identify concepts and content which they map onto the curriculum. In my terms, they show us how to "imagine up" and then to "engineer back down again".

This might be a rallying call, but it is a very responsible one which recognises that our role as educators is not only to inform, but also to engage and inspire. Fundamentally, it is a book that sees and makes the links between all three ambitions.

Give yourself a treat – read it and come away recharged, re-equipped and reaffirmed in your commitment to offer learners a richer and more effective experience in your classes. You can't ask for much more than that!

David Cameron, Kirkcaldy, Fife

acknowledgements

giants' shoulders

We first met on a Saturday in 2004, at a training day with Dorothy Heathcote. Hywel was Jack, Debra was Jill. We've been rolling down hills ever since. Matthew Milburn, then head of Kingstone School in Barnsley, was looking to set up a new Key Stage 3 curriculum which would offer a bridge between the primary and secondary phases and would give children a dilemma-led, humane learning experience. He asked Debra to set it up and to train the staff in the pedagogical approach that would bring the curriculum to life. Hywel was an AST at the school and, over the next two years, the staff who devised and delivered that cultural studies curriculum led a pedagogical revolution across the school that had a significant impact not just on results but on the attitudes and confidence of staff and learners alike. We've not looked back. We owe Matthew and other members of that team – particularly Ondrie Mann and Jane Hewitt – our careers. And, of course, we must also acknowledge the formidable, knowledgeable, compassionate and uncompromisingly rigorous Dorothy Heathcote – the best teacher either of us has ever known.

We both started out as English teachers in the 1990s and, like many English teachers, we ended up also teaching and loving drama. But drama teaching is very specific – it isn't an offshoot of English. It demands a skill set and knowledge base that is broad, both practical and theoretical and also deeply emotional. We needed training. We both remain thankful to the National Association for the Teaching of Drama (NATD) for offering that training and we would like to raise a glass to professional subject bodies everywhere, who hold up their members with support, advice, subject knowledge and more. And to those veteran practitioners, in particular Luke Abbott, who taught us how to look, how to think, how to listen and how to be our authentic selves: thank you.

There be images in this book and neither one of us could have produced these. To Gabriel Kidd, who created them while juggling his A levels, thank you. And to Ian

Gilbert who saw potential in us both some years ago and encouraged us to write, thanks to you too.

No one succeeds alone. This work is credited to the thousands of children, teachers, teaching assistants and leaders who have let us be the teachers we are and who have encouraged us at every step. Thank you.

And finally to our families. For holding back the eye-rolling and the sighs; for picking up the endless domestic duties; for putting up with our bad jokes; for patiently asking the same question ten times before it got through to our daydreaming heads. To Maria, Cath, Tommy, Allan, Joe, Gabriel, Sam – the most patient giants in town – thank you.

CONTENTS

INTRODUCTION

a STATEMENT OF INTENT

Dear parents, teachers, educators and children,

Teachers can't possibly work harder. Schools can't possibly do more. As hard as they may try to, and in spite of all this effort, results don't improve and our children and teachers' mental health suffers. Outside of education, our planet is facing challenges that only the best kinds of thinking will be able to fix. Teaching children the best that has been thought and said only takes us so far. It takes us into our rich and fascinating past. But the future will demand the best that is yet to be said, yet to be thought and yet to be done. That thinking and that action will be done by our children and in order to equip them with the capacity, belief and desire to engage with this, we need to look to the future – empowering children with the belief that they can be agents for change, armed with the tools to imagine themselves into a more humane, creative world.

So this book is an unabashed call to arms for the imagination. For of all the unique attributes of humankind, it is the *imagination* that elevates us to a place where possibilities can become probabilities: to a place of hope. And as teachers, parents and carers of children, what are we if not architects of hope?

Dr Debra Kidd
Hywel Roberts

some routes to the roots
of thinking and learning

Warriors of wonder, let's begin.

This is a book of prompts, provocations and possibilities designed to nourish your creativity and generate ideas that get you excited about learning. It invites a reassessment of what curriculum coverage can look like in the classroom, or even in the home. Rest assured that all the ideas in this book are rooted in practice and grounded in research and have been held up to the scrutiny of professionals across the planet. We want to share with you these routes to joy, warmth, enrichment and progress in the classroom, and we have set the book out accordingly. These are not knowledge organisers or schemes of work; they are inspirational tickles – ideas to get you and your children frothing at the mouth with a sense of purpose while motivating learners to acquire, interpret and apply knowledge and use it to solve problems. Whether you are in an early years setting or a secondary geography classroom, there are adaptable possibilities woven throughout each chapter that place learners, of whatever age, knee-deep in *dilemma*, so that they are thinking deeply, analytically and imaginatively.

Each chapter begins with an image that can be used as a hook into learning in its own right. There are story starters and questions attached to the image to stimulate the imagination and provoke discussion and writing. In addition, each chapter is packed with starting points and "what ifs …?" to establish rich contexts and scenarios for exploration, supported by inductive questioning. We explore these contexts using a variety of approaches, including several drama techniques. For the uninitiated, these appear in bold and are outlined in a list in the back of the book.

Each chapter focuses on a different place. This location is the space our learning will inhabit, where it will be applied and challenged. This *imagined* context, as fantastical as it may appear, will always have the real world as its destination, and the curriculum – as much of it as you wish to explore – sits there, waiting to be discovered. These places are imagined in your classroom, but we would urge you to link them to tangible, lived experiences by taking children out into real forests and caves, mountains and castles, zoos and theme parks. There is a world of curriculum in each of these places. Although we develop a single idea in more detail in each chapter, this is meant to stimulate your own thoughts and imagination and to liberate you from the same old, same old. Be brave!

In this time of high-stakes testing, growing mental health issues among young people, increasing pressure on teachers to focus not on engagement and relevance in learning but instead on rote repetition, practice papers and panic, we have to step back and ask the question, "What is the purpose of education?" If you think it is to get children through tests, then this book is probably not for you. If you think it is to develop wisdom in children – the capacity to think, to apply knowledge, to empathise, to weigh up evidence, to consider consequences and to make informed choices – then this book is most definitely for you.

It is our firm belief, rooted in over 40 years of collective experience, that the most successful schools see examinations as by-products of a great education – not as the end product. They see that education itself is a much more complex journey into the heart of what it is to be human. To reflect that journey, we have organised this book as a series of maps and guides. They are concept and inquiry driven and dovetail beautifully with the Primary Years Programme (PYP) and Middle Years Programme (MYP) of the International Baccalaureate (IB). We've used our native UK terminology of primary, secondary and key stages throughout, but the ideas here are in no way tied to one country or system of education.[1] It is our hope that whatever your context or setting you'll find adaptable ideas that will work in your classroom – this exploration has no borders. No curriculum is so restrictive that this kind of work can't take hold. You just need a good guide book. And here it is.

In each chapter you will find:

The Key

This is an image and a related story starter. It introduces our location and poses some provocative initial questions. It can be used as a stand-alone thinking exercise or as part of the routes to learning – it's up to you. At the

1 For quick reference, Key Stage 3 is roughly equivalent with the US middle school or junior high and the first half of the IB MYP.

very least, it should fire the children's imaginations and stimulate ideas for exploration and writing. Each illustration is available to download from www. crownhouse.co.uk/featured/uncharted-territories so you can use these as prompts for discussion, role play or writing – or anything else that takes your imagination – with your classes.

PRIMARY LANDMARKS

This is a list of potential starting points and ideas which can be used in a primary classroom. We might call them "hooks" or "lures", both of which are not intended to entice children into learning, but to induct them into deep thinking. It's not about coating a strawberry in chocolate – using something as a distraction from the learning – it's about appreciating the strawberry itself – focusing on the underlying substance. Each landmark is linked to an overarching concept and line of inquiry, but these are simply suggestions and you are free to find your own.

SECONDARY LANDMARKS

This is a list of starting points, similar to the primary landmarks but for the secondary classroom, with a slightly greater emphasis on subject-related focus points and ideas. We have tried, as far as possible, to avoid tying these to particular subjects in the hope that some of these sections might encourage interdisciplinary learning opportunities, but we know that canny subject specialists will tune into the elements relevant to their teaching and, in any case, all of these ideas can be adapted for or linked to many different disciplines.

A STOPOVER

This is a more in-depth account of a learning journey, offering transferable ideas that can be adjusted to work with whatever age group you teach. What we're saying is, just because an idea might appear more appropriate for a primary class, and you teach secondary (or vice versa), you should not necessarily discount it. The ideas and concepts – and some of the tasks and techniques – can be filtered and transferred in a number of situations and settings.

STEPPING STONES

These are context-based tasks that you could carry out with your children. They are also included to prod your professional imagination and to explore how elements of, for example, literacy and/or numeracy could be incorporated into the scenario in order to save curriculum time.

THE BEDROCK

This is the *why* of what we are offering in each example: a debrief of the processes and the theoretical and academic underpinning. Just in case anyone asks. It's critical that, as teachers, we understand why we do what we do and that we're able to justify it when questioned. The bedrock sections give you more detailed information about learning and the underpinning research.

The real driver that prompted us to write this book was the hundreds of inspirational teachers we have worked with who have found that, in recent years, their own creativity has been stifled somewhat by the fog of bureaucracy and the narrowing of the curriculum offer. A rising fear of not *covering the content of the curriculum* and of hit-or-miss inspections has led to a shortening of that list of strategies deemed "the right way". Rather than seeing teachers as trainers of children, we would rather think of ourselves as Sherpas of the curriculum and that's why we've shaped the book in the way we have.

So, take our hands and walk with us. There may be dragons.

Chapter 1

The Forest

All the stories were gathered here, in one place.

Why is the figure in the forest?

Will the trees protect the forest visitor?

Where next for this forest visitor?

Is this a secret place?

Why might trees not like books?

Can a tree weep?

What else have the trees witnessed?

Who sits in the light, gathering the books?

Is the book we see in the distance coming towards us, or being sucked away?

Your own questions ...

the forest

There are few places as magical as a forest. Whether we think of fairy tales – like Hansel and Gretel – of poetry, or of walking through woods on snowy nights, forests are places of intrigue, mystery and quite possibly danger. In the real world and on a practical level, we need forests, and exploring why can be a key area of learning. Topics to explore could include understanding the role forests play in producing oxygen for human beings, in keeping ecosystems in balance and in providing habitats for animal species. So step onto the path and enter the forest …

primary landmarks

⊙ **What if …** the children are brought into the forest to meet the Fairy King, Oberon, who tells the children that in his kingdom, there is a thief who is stealing children and fairy folk? He takes them, leaving behind only their shadows. The forest is full of these sad, lost shadows. Could the children create the shadows using screens and lights? Can they find the thief and reunite the shadows with their owners? They may need to make a mental or physical map of the forest – the troll caves, the pondering ponds and all kinds of other places spinning from their imaginations – in order to finish the story. They could also consider other stories where shadows are separated from their owners – for example, Peter Pan.

Concept: Light and shadow.

Lines of inquiry: Why are forests such common settings in traditional stories? What do story settings tell us about the relationship between humankind and nature? What kinds of mythical creatures do we find in forests? What are shadows and how are they formed?

Curriculum areas: Geographical mapping, science investigations – shadows and light, literacy, narrative inquiry, story creation.

◐ **What if ...** the children, in role as surveyors, were asked to inspect and write a report on a derelict Gothic property, hidden deep in the forest? The children are only told that the report should be positive and that the client is a rich man who lives abroad. If he buys the property, they will receive a fee. To entice them in, you can use an image of an abandoned house in a forest. The property has been empty for many, many years. They enter the forest on a dark, dreary day. Having mapped out the house, describing the rooms, they write a full report, describing the house in as positive a light as they can. But then, they receive a letter from their client, who is revealed as none other than Count Dracula ... He is looking forward to receiving their report and is keen to purchase a new home. But do they really want Count Dracula to move into the forest? What about the other people living there? Would he be a danger to them? What should they do next? How can they put him off? Or would they sell the house and take the fee?

Concept: Public interest.

Lines of inquiry: Is the customer always right? Are there some circumstances in which we have a duty to say no? How do you say no to someone who is more powerful than you?

Curriculum areas: Geographical mapping, producing scaled drawings (area, scale and ratio), report writing, measuring, Gothic literature, letter writing, problem solving.

◐ **What if ...** Little Red Riding Hood, months after her trauma with the wolf, is too frightened to venture outside? Her friends are worried about her. They decide they must go into the forest to seek out the wolf's family in an attempt to negotiate a restorative conversation between their friend and the wolves. But they find, to their surprise, that the wolves are also too scared to leave their lair after the incident. How can peace be restored in the forest? Is it possible for the wolves and the humans to coexist in this habitat? Could we create a safe habitat for the wolves so they are kept away from the humans?

Concept: Restorative justice.

Lines of inquiry: How do we help people to recover from bad events? What responsibility do we bear for our friends' and family's actions? Can we change our nature?

Curriculum areas: Restorative talk, negotiating, mapping, exploring natural habitats, protecting different species and humans, conservation.

◎ **What if …** you discover that the class teddy bear has gone missing? You find a note which says that he has gone to find his family in the deep, dark forest. You are worried about him – the forest is magical but there are many dangers in it. Should you go and help him? What will you need to take? How can you talk to the trees so that they will help you and see you as their friends?

Concept: Helping others.

Lines of inquiry: Is it ever right to put yourself in danger in order to help a friend? What should we take into a forest to keep us safe? What might we find in the forest? How will we find our way home again?

Curriculum areas: Communication and language, personal, social and emotional development, numeracy, counting and mapping, literacy, making labels to guide the way home, designing homes for magical creatures in the forest, making habitats for real ones.

◎ **What if …** all the books in the world were disappearing into a magical forest? Who might want them and why? How might you find out what is happening? Dare you venture into the Forest of Fearsome Faces in order to discover more?

Concept: Cultural heritage.

Lines of inquiry: Why do books matter? Which are the best kinds of books? Where do books come from and what do they have to do with trees? Could you use the image at the beginning of the chapter to create your own book? What if the image were the first in a book? What if it were in the middle? What if it were at the end? How would this influence the narrative structure?

Curriculum areas: Literacy, reading favourite books, writing (Could the children collectively write a book and track it to see where the book thief is going with all the books?), oracy (How will they persuade the book thief to give the books back?).

secondary landmarks

⊙ **What if ...** you were scientists or botanists, whose job it was to collect rare plants used in medicines? What kind of forest might you be sent to? What might be the threats to this forest? Can the ingredients for the medicines be synthetically manufactured rather than taken from plants? Is there anything you can do to make sure that precious plants are conserved? Are some plants more deserving of conservation than others?

Concept: Conservation.

Lines of inquiry: Why do we need plants and whose responsibility is it to conserve them? Would it ever be right for someone to "own" a species of plant?

Curriculum areas: Ethics, biology, conservation, geography, business.

⊙ **What if ...** this were the last remaining forest in the world and you were charged with the responsibility of taking care of it? In addition to managing the footpaths and caring for the different plants and animals, you need to manage the number of tourists and create multilingual resources for them. You will have to work out how many visitors you can cope with, balancing the need to generate income to help conserve the forest with the need to protect the forest from the harm caused by too many people. What if a new leader is voted into office who decides the forest should go?

Concept: Conservation and tourism.

Lines of inquiry: How can we balance protecting our natural wonders with allowing people to visit and appreciate them? How do conservation organisations receive funding in order to do their work?

Curriculum areas: Conservation of forest areas, mapping, budgeting, planning, designing, drawing to scale, political negotiation and protest, writing to inform and persuade.

⊙ **What if ...** you were Khejarli villagers in a forest in 1730? These villagers were part of a Hindu sect, committed to protecting the trees, plants and animals around them, which they viewed as being part of a sacred whole. When the Maharaja's army came to cut down the trees, they stood in the way to protect them, despite the threat of violence. How might this decision have been made? What kind of belief system would you need to have to be willing to sacrifice your own life for a tree? What kinds of prayers, rituals and conversations might these people have had? What went through their minds when the soldiers came and cut down their people along with the trees? Tragically, 363 people died in this way. When we look at what we know today about climate change and the importance of trees to our health, do their actions have extra significance? Were they foolish to sacrifice their lives for this cause?

Concept: Beliefs and values.

Lines of inquiry: Is anything worth dying for? How do we speak to power? How might diplomacy work in order to avoid tragedy?

Curriculum areas: Religion, history of branches of Hinduism, the roots of the conservation movement, power and control in hierarchical systems, ethics, beliefs and philosophy, language and power.

a stopover

This session was originally taught to Year 4 children but could easily be adapted for older classes.

The children enter the room to find a large circle made of masking tape, which represents an oak tree. You may want to cut some oak leaf shapes out of paper and scatter them around. If you can source them, you could add some acorns. Projected onto the wall is an image of a forest. Begin by talking about the forest:

"What if we imagine we have lived in this forest for all of our lives? And that those lives were lived a very long time ago – over 400 years ago. What might our lives have been like? What kinds of jobs might we have done?"

Let the children create **occupational mimes** of the jobs they could do and discuss them before continuing:

"We have lived here for so long, we have had time to think of names for all of the trees. They mean something to us all. Can we all please stand up and think of a name for our favourite tree ... maybe 'the tree of wishes' or 'the story tree'. What would you call yours?"

Get the children to name their tree – building investment in the forest and the trees that inhabit it. Build their names into stories – for example, "Ah – the tree of playfulness – this is where all the children come to ... Oh ... the tree of curiosity! It is said that this tree can whisper secrets to you when the wind is blowing from the north ..." You can, if you like, get the children to create their own stories about their trees and what makes them special.

Once the children have named the forest and built the stories of the trees, bring them to the circle you have created with masking tape and reveal that this represents a tree. Scrunched up and thrown away some distance from the circle, is a piece of parchment paper with old-fashioned writing on it. The children won't find this paper straight away, but on it, in Latin, are written these words:

"Credo in unum Deum. Patrem omnipotentem factorem caeli et terrae, visibilium, omnium et invisibilium."

This translates as: "I believe in one God. The Father almighty, maker of heaven and earth, and of all things visible and invisible." Close to where you've discarded the parchment, on the nearest wall, place a piece of paper with a crucifix drawn on it. You'll need both of these later.

Seat them around the masking tape and say, "Can we agree that this circle represents the largest tree in this great forest? The biggest tree of them all."

Talk with the children about the tree – to be this large, how old must it be? How could we find out? If they suggest chopping it down to count the rings, say it would be a shame to destroy it just to find out its age – could there be another way? Let the children suggest ideas. They may suggest measuring the circumference and researching other trees of a similar size. They may suggest asking the tree. You could try both ideas. They may say nothing at all. In which case, you can question:

"I wonder if there are other trees in the world which are the same size as this one. I wonder whether we could make a good guess about how old our tree is if we knew how old they are. How might we measure our tree so we know how big it is?"

You may choose to use a calculation. One way of calculating the age of a tree is to measure the tree's circumference, calculate the diameter and then multiply this by the average growth factor for the species. There are various guides available on the internet which explain how to do this in more detail – the wikihow one is quite useful.[1] The Woodland Trust also have a useful resource for approximating the age of an oak from its size.[2] A circumference of around 7.5m will make your tree roughly 600 years old. If you want an older tree, make your circle bigger. If younger, make it smaller.

Once the children have established the estimated age of the tree, you can create a timeline. You can make a timeline using a long strip of border paper, lining paper or masking tape. Get the children to write down important events and dates which took place during the tree's lifetime. What might this tree have witnessed in human history? Now let's imagine that we are sitting around this tree, not in our time, but in 1580. Putting ourselves in the past with the tree, can we imagine what the tree might be able to see? How much further back could we go? Can we add more events to our timeline now? When on our timeline would the tree have been seeded? You could ask the children to discuss or to begin to write a description of some of the things the tree might have seen, heard and felt in its lifetime. This can be spoken or written – you are building investment in the tree so that they begin to care about it and to develop a sense of the scale of its lifetime. They might like to research some of these events. Why might there be some decades, or even centuries, that we seem to know very little about? Which periods of history do we seem to know most about? Why? You might lead the discussion to look at when the printing press was invented and how this made it easier to record and share ideas and information. To what extent is our knowledge of history affected by the records that people have left behind? What kinds of records do we use to learn about people's lives if we don't have written information? What kind of record might this tree leave? Does the fact that the tree cannot tell us its history make it less important than someone who can speak? Why not write some of its history? This could be factual or sensory descriptive writing.

....

1 See https://www.wikihow.com/Determine-the-Age-of-a-Tree.
2 See http://www.wbrc.org.uk/atp/Estimating%20Age%20of%20Oaks%20-%20Woodland%20Trust. pdf.

Remind the children of their occupational mimes and revisit them. Explain that you are about to enter into a story. It is 1580 and they live and work in this magnificent forest. At this point in the story, they have just finished work and would normally be heading home for the day, but someone wants to see them first …

"Now that we understand the kind of time we are living in and the tools we have to hand, we are going to meet someone who has asked us to do a job for him. He wants to meet us by the old tree. He has asked to meet us at dusk when the forest will be almost dark."

You could soundscape the forest at this time. How does the forest feel as night-time approaches? What can the children hear?

The teacher prepares the children for role play:

"When I step forward, can we agree that I am speaking as a nobleman? A man who has just arrived in this place, but one who now has power over us? Can we agree that this man owns the land on which we work and on which our cottages stand? Can we agree that this man has the power to let us stay in our homes or to force us to leave our dwellings and our village? Good – then let's step into our story."

Use **teacher in role** to deliver the nobleman's words:

"Good evening, all. It is pleasing to see all the villagers in attendance. As you know, I am the proud landowner of this forest – part of a gift of land bequeathed to me by our great Queen Elizabeth. It is my intention to honour our queen by constructing, at the edge of this vast forest, a house so spectacular that she cannot but wish to visit it. It will be built in the shape of an E, to honour her name. And the entrance to this house will be marked by the most magnificent of doors – a door made of the finest English oak. A door made from the greatest tree in the forest – this mighty English oak, next to which we stand gathered on this fine evening."

Let the children react – draw them into conversation – and see if you can tempt them to challenge you and offer reasons why they think you should not cut down this tree. If they are not stepping forward or engaging, step out of the story:

"Stepping out of the story for the moment – back to the present and our classroom – what just happened? Who was that man? What did he want? What do we think the villagers should do?"

Let the children ponder the problem and offer some ideas before returning to roles and playing them out. You, as the landowner in the piece, are not going to make it easy for them. If they refuse to let you cut down the tree, you threaten them and their families with eviction and destitution. You may even threaten that you will tell the queen of their disrespect. Put them in a pickle. They don't want to cut down the tree, but they seem to have little choice. Place blocks at every turn – if they suggest the tree is cursed, accuse them of witchcraft and threaten to report them to the authorities. If they suggest that the tree is diseased, say they should cut it down anyway in that case in order to halt the spread of infection. If they (rightly) point out that a tree this age is hollowing and won't make a good door, ask them to select which tree to use from the ones they named earlier. You are creating a mind maze in which each turn they try to take is blocked with more difficulty. When they seem to have run out of direct challenges, end, in role, with this:

"Good. 'Tis decided then. I shall leave you to work out how it shall be done. And there will be a handsome reward for all of you, should you be able to ensure that the felled tree falls in that direction – onto the old Catholic chapel. The reward will be handsome, but your silence will be expected. It must appear as if it were an accident – an error. The queen is clear that she does not wish the Catholics to be provoked in her name. But I need to build a new road. And *that* building is in my way!"

Step out of the story again and unpick this latest twist with the children. Turn to "look" at the chapel and, together, start to build a description of it. Ask the children to add ideas to the picture:

"I can see …"

Old stone walls

Moss growing over the steps

A wooden door

Windows covered with grime

A cracked pane of glass

Ask the children if they think you should all go over to the chapel to have a look at what's inside. What might you find? You may discover an old key. You may discover a discarded note from a mass – the piece of scrunched-up paper with the Latin writing on it. What do these words mean? What do we know about Catholics at this time in history? Why might the queen want to keep the peace with the Catholics? What has happened? You might take some time out to explore the context before going any further. You might want the children to learn about the kinds of objects and artefacts they are likely to find in a Catholic chapel. You might want them to do a little research into the Catholic mass. Once they have gathered or been taught the knowledge they need, you can re-enter the story.

Gather the children at the entrance to the chapel. Open the door – let them create the sound of the old door opening.

"The inside is so dark. The shafts of light coming through the windows are casting such strange shadows in the gloomy interior. Dust is dancing in the light beams. And here and there, notice the light glimmering on objects made of gold – a chalice, icons painted in gold leaf, the lettering on a bible."

Get the children to label the space using sticky notes. They write down the name of an object and place it in the space where they think it would be. Then you add your own. On your note is written, "Breadcrumbs and a half-full cup of water."

Place it somewhere subtly. When you come to look at what everyone has written, draw the children's attention to this note. What can we infer from it?

Explain to the children that you now have two problems. You have been asked to cut down a tree, which you want to protect. Then you find out you are meant to make the tree fall onto a building where it seems someone is taking shelter. What should you do?

What comes next will depend on the children's decisions, but there is a world of activity you could explore:

- They could seek to speak with the priest and find out what happened and why he is hiding in the chapel? Why might he not feel safe to come out? Was Elizabethan England really safe for Catholics after the uprising of 1569 and the Papal Bull of 1570? Was he involved? Is there a history between him and some of the older villagers? Could you find a way to make him safe?

- They could write to the queen, pleading for intervention, clarification or reassurances. They could try to persuade the priest to vow allegiance to the queen.

- They could try to persuade the landowner that another road could be grander. They would need to map and design their ideas, using other stately entrances and driveways as examples.

- They could warn the priest and fell the tree. How would you cut a tree of this size down with the tools available at the time? How would you make it fall in a certain direction?

- They could speak to other villagers who remember the old priest and the old chapel – it may be that many of them were once Catholic – before King Henry VIII forced them to convert. It could be that, even to this day, some of them resent being forced to change religion – or resent the priest's reaction when they did. The children could write about this in character.

- They could apologise to the priest and warn him that the chapel is to be destroyed, but promise to try to protect the precious frescos, windows and artefacts in it. How? What could they do with them? Do they belong to the landowner now and, if so, is protecting them a form of theft?

The children could write up a story of the events that have unfolded from the point of view of either the landowner, the priest or the woodcutters. How will history judge them?

This is just one possible route through the forest. There are many, many more – think of the magical woods of Shakespeare's *A Midsummer Night's Dream* or the silent snowy woodland of Robert Frost's poem, "Stopping by Woods on a Snowy Evening". Think of a rainforest and an undiscovered tribe in danger of losing their home to deforestation. Think of a forest in a mythical land, a forest in which the faces of lost souls appear in the bark of the trees. Think of a forest in which slithy toves and Jabberwocks lurk. Think of a forest where paths diverge: which one will you choose? Whichever you follow, you'll find the curriculum opening up before you.

stepping stones

You could:

- Research ancient trees and find out more about the lifespans of trees.
- Debate whether we should be allowed to cut down trees.
- Design protected areas for dangerous parts of the forest. Why might some areas of the forest be dangerous?
- Find out which creatures live in the tree and consider how felling the tree might affect them.
- Design new homes or habitats for the creatures displaced from the tree.
- Design a guided forest walk, perhaps with directions in more than one language.
- Compare the lifespan of the trees to the lifespan of the animals and creatures (including human beings) that live in the forest.
- Learn about how the Woodland Trust and other organisations maintain their land and the kinds of tasks people who work for them carry out.

- Read poems describing forests and create soundscapes and soundtracks to accompany them, leading to a performance.
- Visit a forest.

The Bedrock – Manipulating Knowledge

This way of working may seem to directly challenge the "just tell them" school of thought, but it is not intended to offer a "fluffy" alternative to knowledge – rather it encourages us to think more deeply about how we can ensure that children use knowledge in shifting circumstances and in situations where they may encounter the unexpected. When entering contexts for learning such as these, it's sometimes necessary to step out of the fiction or story in order to "deliver" key information so that the narrative or the problem solving can progress. When exploring the age of the tree, for example, you may want to teach the children some relevant maths in order for them to do their calculations. It's perfectly fine to step in and out of the fiction as you see fit and to discretely teach the children whatever knowledge they are going to need. Similarly, if the children decide they should write to the queen, they need to be taught how to write a good letter and how to lay it out. The knowledge is still explicitly taught, but you are doing this within the context of a clear sense of purpose. Feeling that something has significance and value is a powerful motivating force for human beings.[3]

There is little doubt that, at the time of writing, the examination system at both primary and secondary level in England is increasingly focused on "catching children out" by giving them unexpected scenarios or by disguising key knowledge in unfamiliar contexts. Internationally, we know that one focus of PISA tests is the application of knowledge in unfamiliar, global contexts – a focus too for the IB's programmes. As such, we need to ensure that pupils are not fazed by such trickery in exams. Being able to override the panic which arises from the unexpected is a form of self-regulation, one of the traits that the Education Endowment Foundation (EEF) Toolkit rates highly in terms of impact on pupil outcomes (+8

---

3 Pink, D. (2009) *Drive: The Surprising Truth About What Motivates Us*. New York: Riverhead.

months of benefit in terms of progress) yet there is little guidance as to how we develop self-regulation in others.[4]

Perhaps one way to do this is to immerse the children in the unfamiliar, the unexpected and the difficult from the word go, while not losing the opportunity to engage them in imaginative contexts. We *could* give them harder tests, or we could give them more demanding contexts that will be memorable. Research by cognitive scientists tells us that stories are privileged in our minds – capitalising on this by creating narrative contexts for learning can be hugely beneficial.[5] We cover this further later in the book.

Much of what has been written on memory in relation to educational research has focused very specifically on learning with regard to testing, particularly in the more market driven educational settings found in the US and the UK. The "what works" agenda looks very closely at how to get information to stick through a process of deliberate and spaced practice so that it can be held securely for a test. While there is no doubt that these techniques work, they nevertheless betray a limited view of memory and of learning. Exponents of these techniques attempt, in effect, to bypass consideration of motivation, emotional engagement, multisensory learning and higher order thinking skills, and effectively make the case that learning need not be interesting or rewarding, as long as it achieves the outcomes we value in a test-based culture. For anyone who views education as something more than simply passing tests – for those pursuing the idea of "warmth" in the curriculum, as outlined in the introduction – this view of memory is rather limited.

Instead, we may choose to look more widely at the work on memory and link this to notions of value and purpose. For example, recent work on embodied cognition shows a much more complex interplay between mind and body than was previously accepted.[6] As Professor Guy Claxton shows in his detailed analysis of the research into embodied cognition, our memory is closely interwoven with our

---

4 The Education Endowment Foundation Toolkit. Available at: https://educationendowmentfoundation.org.uk/resources/teaching-learning-toolkit.

5 Willingham, D. (2004) Ask the cognitive scientist: the privileged status of story, *American Educator.* Available at: http://www.aft.org/periodical/american-educator/summer-2004/ask-cognitive-scientist.

6 Claxton, G. (2016) *Intelligence in the Flesh: Why Your Mind Needs Your Body Much More Than It Thinks.* New Haven, CT: Yale University Press.

physiological self and we would do well to consider the importance of movement in learning.

Indeed, the importance of movement and free play is central to learning in early childhood, as indicated by research suggesting that formal learning, when introduced before the age of 7, can be detrimental to concentration and self-regulation when measured at the age of 11.[7] In countries with lower recorded levels of attention deficit hyperactivity disorder (ADHD), starting dates for formal education tend to be later and high-quality, active, play-based preschool education is typically in place. In these settings, the emphasis placed on activity, imagination and play is deemed crucial in creating focused and agentive learners. Even beyond the age of 7, the benefits of playfulness, imaginative endeavour and movement are well-documented.[8] To reduce learning to a static, repetitive activity is to reduce children's experience of life; a view of education that we strongly resist.

As we go through these bedrock sections, we'll build on the importance of purpose and play by exploring the roles of talk, imagination, empathy, creativity, emotion and moral purpose. And we'll ask, what would a "whole" education look like – one that seeks to shape the heart, mind and body, without treating them as separate entities?

7   Dee, T. S. and Sievertsen, H. H. (2015) *The Gift of Time? School Starting Age and Mental Health*, NBER Working Paper No. 21610. Cambridge, MA: The National Bureau of Economic Research. Available at: http://www.nber.org/papers/w21610.
8   Bateson, P. and Martin, P. (2013) *Play, Playfulness, Creativity and Innovation*. Cambridge: Cambridge University Press.

chapter 2

The castle

And here was the destination at last.
But would their promises be kept?

What is written in the stars?

Who designed the castle?

Where are we?

What year is it?

Who might be looking at us from the window and what might they be thinking?

Is the small, white figure safe?

There is a bridge from the castle to the place where we are standing. Where are we standing and what brought us to this place?

Does the castle have a name?

Your own questions ...

_____

_____

_____

_____

Download the image from www.crownhouse.co.uk/featured/uncharted-territories

The castle

From forests, we move to castles – humans making their impression on the landscape. From history to fantasy, castles are writ large in our cultural heritage. Defensive or aggressive? Magical or cold? From warfare and sieges to princesses and dragons, we explore the richness of these fascinating places.

Primary Landmarks

⊙ **What if ...** you were a team of paranormal investigators called to investigate a strange phenomenon? During the daytime, there is no castle beside the lake. But at nightfall, it appears. Witnesses describe a sound coming from the castle – the whistling of a mournful tune. Others have seen what appears to be a face peering out of an upstairs window. At night the phantom castle is separated from the land by a shimmering moat, but no one has ever crossed it. Until …

Concept: Myths and legends.

Lines of inquiry: How do myths develop? Are they ever rooted in reality? What conventions of ghost stories are evident in this story setting?

Curriculum areas: Critical thinking, fact and fiction, unexplained phenomena and beliefs, story writing, Gothic literary conventions, drawing or creating the imagined setting.

⊙ **What if ...** you were a team of castle designers in medieval times? A Norman nobleman has asked you to design an impenetrable castle for him. He fears invasion and wants the castle to be able to withstand a siege that might last for over a year. What would you need in the castle? How would you keep people out? You need to think about food supplies, communication with the outside world, defence (and self-defence), warmth, sanitation and habitation. What kind of location would you choose for your castle?

Concept: Heritage.

Lines of inquiry: Who lived in castles and why? Where were castles most likely to be built and why? Were castles successful in protecting people or did they simply attract attack and cause suffering?

Curriculum areas: The Norman period, life in medieval castles, sieges and attacks, defence and survival tactics, scaled drawings of castles, diary extracts, numeracy, rationing and food supplies.

◉ **What if ...** you receive a letter from the king? His daughter has been captured and is being held in a castle by a dragon. The dragon wants all the king's treasure and will not let the princess go until he has it. But the king is a greedy man. He wants his daughter returned but he does not want to lose his treasure. He writes to you, his knights and knightesses, and asks you to plan a daring rescue. What will you need to take with you? How will you get in? You'll need plans of the castle and you'll need a good understanding of dragons. You'll need to be clever and brave. What if, when you get there, you find out that the dragon and the princess are now friends and that she wants to stay? Will you risk the wrath of the king or the wrath of the dragon?

Concept: Greed.

Lines of inquiry: Are human beings better than animals? What makes someone or something likeable? Why might we harm something we fear, if it is not a danger to us? Is it possible to change your mind about someone?

Curriculum areas: Planning and designing a route, mapping and scale, descriptive writing, writing persuasive pieces, oracy skills, negotiating.

secondary landmarks

◉ **What if ...** you were called in by the local tourist office to help them promote visits to a local castle? They are concerned that visitor numbers have dropped off and that, although the castle has a great history, all people see when they arrive is a heap of stones. There is a great bottle dungeon, but people just throw rubbish into it. The great hall is full of toddlers running around. It is stark and unfurnished and no one seems to be able to imagine how it might once have been. The tourist office has asked you to create re-enactments, projections and displays in order to bring the history of this castle to life. (You could adapt this idea using a castle in your local area or invent one.)

Concept: Conservation and cultural heritage.

Lines of inquiry: How can historical sites compete with technology for our attention? How can we make people appreciate our heritage? How can we bring history to life?

Curriculum areas: Writing engaging and informative texts, using technology, photography and models to create informative and exciting displays, ensuring our historical knowledge is accurate, promoting and publicising our work, designing promotional materials.

⊙ **What if ...** you were a team of interior and landscape designers? A local castle has been bought by a businesswoman who wants to turn it into a hotel. There are planning restrictions on the castle as it is a listed building. There have also been objections from local people, so the owner is keen that the design remains sympathetic to the castle's origins, while being modern and comfortable. How would you design the guest rooms and public spaces? What about the design of the garden? Where would the car park go so as not to obscure the views? What kind of furniture would you source? What would go on the walls? What is your budget? In each room, the owner would like an information plaque describing design concept, linking this to an aspect of history of the castle. You will need to research, write and design this plaque. What if there was a rumour of a ghost? Would you incorporate it into your designs or ignore it?

Concept: Restoration, old versus new.

Lines of inquiry: How can we honour our past while creating modern comfort for visitors? How do hotels work? What is an interior designer and what is their design process? How can we inform guests about the hotel's past without making it feel like a museum? What extra facilities and rooms would we have that weren't in the original building? Where would they go?

Curriculum areas: Design, textiles, leisure and tourism, budgeting, writing to inform.

⊙ **What if ...** you were asked to create an exhibition for visitors to the site of one of the sieges of the English Civil War? You could choose Newark,

Scarborough, York, Bradford or any other. As well as simply being offered information, visitors need to be able to understand the impact of sieges in an emotional way. How could you get visitors to care about and empathise with the people affected? The visitors should understand the causes and consequences of the siege and its effect on the outcome of the war. The exhibition should introduce visitors to what the civil war was, how it came about and how it impacted on the people of Britain.

Concept: Conflict and the impact on ordinary people.

Lines of inquiry: Who suffers most in war? If you were starving, what lengths would you go to in order to survive? Who is to blame for the death of civilians in war? How are sieges used to win wars? (You could compare these historic siege situations with the current sieges taking place in Syria.)

Curriculum areas: History of the English Civil War, impact on people who are besieged, planning for a siege, food and the human body, nutritional needs, the impact of starvation, starvation as a weapon in war.

a stopover

This was originally devised for a secondary English class, but could also be used for media studies. It would be most suitable for Key Stage 3 (11–14-year-olds), but could easily be adapted for older groups.

Using the poem "Christabel" by Samuel Taylor Coleridge, the children could look at how a film director and crew might bring a text to life. Looking at the illustration provided at the start of this chapter and a copy of the poem (available from the Poetry Foundation – https://www.poetryfoundation.org/poems/43971/christabel), the class could consider lighting, location, sound effects, costuming, casting and camera angles. They could take the poem and decide on dialogue and any narration or captioning they might want. They could create a storyboard and film poster.

Begin by gathering the class around and reading the first two stanzas of the poem. What time is it when the owls awaken the crowing cock? What mood is Coleridge trying to create? Look at the illustration of the castle by the lake at the start of this chapter. How would you describe this setting? Let the class talk, then say:

"If this is our location for the filming of this story and we are creating our opening sequence, what would we film and what sounds would we record?"

Get the class to storyboard this opening scene, using either technology or simple pen and paper. Ask them to consider what sound effects they would use in the accompanying soundscape. You might choose to soundscape this using found sound and the children's voices.

Draw their attention to the words "my lady's shroud" at the end of the first stanza. Whose perspective is the tale being told from? Who might the lady be? What is a shroud? Could they extend the deathly imagery by adding a tomb or grave to their storyboard at this point? What would it look like? What mood would it convey? Gather them to share their ideas and ask them what atmosphere they think a film director might want to create. What do they think might be about to happen in the poem? You can discuss the idea of genre and how generic conventions are established early on in a film, novel or poem.

Read the next three stanzas, in which Christabel is walking in the forest, concerned for the well-being of her knight who is far away (presumably engaged in battle – perhaps in the Crusades). Her reverie is interrupted and she is startled. Taking this section, ask one child to play Christabel, standing in the centre, and the other children to take positions around her. Imagine Christabel standing in the woods. She is surrounded by trees and animals. The wind is blowing gently. If each of these things – trees, animals and the wind – could describe her in one line, what would it be? The description should hint at what she is – like a riddle. It should aim to speak of her beauty and of familiarity – this is a place she comes often, where she feels safe. It is a place that knows her well. When the children have written or thought of their line, perform them ceremoniously, as a collective poem. You might decide to shape this further as individual pieces of writing.

You might want to consider the knight for a moment at this point. Where might he be? The children could research the Crusades. Ask them what we would see him doing if, at this point in the film, we were to cut away to a shot of him. They could create **still images** with captions, share and discuss these and then use them as a basis for writing – perhaps a letter from the knight to Christabel.

Read on to the point where Christabel meets Geraldine and offers to take her to the castle. How would this new character be introduced in your film? "It moaned as near, as near can be, But what it is she cannot tell" – how would we create a sense of foreboding and mystery before we see what "it" is? How would Geraldine be lit? How would her "whiteness" and almost ghostliness be shown in film? Do we trust her? How could we sow seeds of doubt in the way we choose to cast and film her? In the image at the start of the chapter, our artist has drawn a serpent in the night sky – can the children find it? What might a serpent suggest? What connotations do they have? Can our future be written in the stars? Why might an artist hint in this way?

Can the children describe the encounter between Christabel and Geraldine, taking on board Coleridge's descriptions of her as beautiful but "strange" with gems "entangled" in her hair. Contrast the description of her with the description of the castle, "The hall as silent as the cell". How is the interior contrasted with the exterior you imagine creating for your film? What might the forest represent in comparison with the grey, stone, forbidding castle? Or with Christabel's father, Sir Leoline, who is "weak in health"? You are introducing the idea of juxtaposition here.

At this stage, can the children guess what the conventions of such a tale may be? A motherless young woman, living in a cold castle with an ailing, grieving father … in walks a beautiful, almost ghostly noble woman … what could possibly happen? Can they act out, using three still images and no more than twenty words, what they think will happen? Alternatively, get the class to write predictions on a piece of paper and save them for later. In the film, if they want to use foreshadowing to hint at their predictions, what might their shots show?

Read the stanza in which Geraldine and Christabel enter the castle and consider the mastiff's reaction:

The mastiff old did not awake,
Yet she an angry moan did make!
And what can ail the mastiff bitch?

It is a generic convention that animals can sense evil or threats when they arrive in the household. What could the dog be dreaming about? What could be ailing the dog to cause this "angry moan"? Does Christabel notice? The children could write their own descriptions of the moment that the woman and Christabel enter the castle, or storyboard this scene. Perhaps they could write a description from the dog's perspective?

The women creep quietly through the castle so as not to wake the weakened Sir Leoline. Could the students model or map the layout of the castle? What is the floor made of? How is it lit? They may need to do some research into what castles looked like in medieval times. How do they contrast with the fantasy castles we see in fairy tales? Which style would they want to use in your film? Could they write a brief for the set designers of what they want to achieve with these inside scenes?

Look at Coleridge's lexical choices here – "steal", "jealous", "gloom", "death" – how could this foreshadowing be shown in images rather than words? What could the film focus on to create this sense of danger and warning? How do Christabel's bare feet make her more vulnerable? At this point, the children could design or describe the costumes the two women are wearing. Could they use design to symbolise the threat that Geraldine poses to Christabel? Could they incorporate some of the key images from the poem?

As you continue to read through the poem, similar tasks can be undertaken so that the children focus in on particular details and think about how to bring them to life in images. They can explore the symbolism of the serpent, the weakness of the Baron, the entrapment of Christabel and the theme of good versus evil. But the story is incomplete. What might happen? How will your film end? Will the children choose to introduce the ghost of Christabel's mother? The knight from battle? Will Christabel find a way to free herself? How would such an ending fit with the role of women and religion in society when the poem was written? What might a modern ending look like? Could the children research Coleridge and his beliefs and imagine an alternative ending he might have wanted to tell? Would Coleridge have been constrained by the time and society in which he was writing, and, if so, how and why? How do moral tales and fairy stories reflect our culture and our values?

stepping stones

You could:

- Create contrasting still images, then and now, of life in and around a castle – both real and the one in the poem.

- Give an account of a day in the life of a servant to a great nobleman – this could be in the form of a diary entry or acted out.

- Debate whether something as ancient as a castle should be preserved or restored.

- Design a vetting procedure to decide who lives within the castle walls and who lives outside. Should these procedures alter in times of war? Are horses more important than people? How do we ensure the availability of fresh water during difficult times such as war or siege?

- Consider what jobs needed to be done in the day-to-day running of a castle in ancient times. How would these jobs change with the arrival of a king or queen?

- Commission the class to design a new coat of arms for a brave knight.

- Visit a castle.

The bedrock – creativity

The stopover in this section explores how you might take literary analysis onto a more creative plane, pulling in design, art, writing, drama and media tasks under the umbrella of English, with the option to use technology where appropriate. It allows children to pull in their existing knowledge of genre while deepening their contextual understanding and allowing them to think about creating something new. During the late 1990s and the first decade of this millennium, much was written about the importance of creativity in terms of schooling and pedagogy.[1]

---

1 National Advisory Committee on Creative and Cultural Education (1999) *All Our Futures: Creativity, Culture and Education.* Available at: http://sirkenrobinson.com/pdf/allourfutures.pdf.

In more recent times, the focus has shifted away from this and onto the mechanics of memory – in particular, working memory and the retention of knowledge. It is now commonly alleged that creativity can only develop in a worthwhile way if knowledge is in place first – the stimulus-organism-response (S-O-R) model in neuroscientific terms.[2] Yet knowledge and creativity can work in tandem and it's not necessarily the case that the former needs to be taught first. Indeed, some neuroscientists are beginning to regard the S-O-R model as deficient in its ability to deal with complexity and with the interplay between body and mind in a creative process.[3] Even if you take the view that prior knowledge is a key element of creativity, an insistence that everything deemed to be important by the teacher must be transmitted first creates the danger of overloading the curriculum with knowledge acquisition, while the opportunity to apply that in a creative context is left to chance. Many who advocate this model simply assume that children will "naturally" apply their creativity. Some will, of course, but many won't. We would not leave reading to chance, or maths. We recognise the need to teach the vital basic skills of literacy and numeracy, and the need to give children as much opportunity for practice as possible. There's a contradiction here if we assume that creativity will simply flow from knowledge.

Creativity requires the imaginative application of knowledge in a new way – making connections between domains and generating something original that carries with it a sense of value. While this general definition of creativity is widely accepted – we have adapted it slightly from NACCCE's (1999) report[4] – the importance of creativity seems to have dropped off policymakers' radars in many Western countries. It is not that knowledge doesn't matter – it matters a great deal – but here we are concerned with what we do with knowledge and how what we *know* can be married with what we can *imagine*.

In the example offered, the children are looking closely at the language of the poem – the lexical choices of the poet, for example – but are doing so in a way that requires them to lift the words off the page and bring them to life in film. To do so, they have to draw on a number of areas of knowledge – literary genre, historical context, technical information about filming and design, and so on.

....

2 Jaccard, J. and Jacoby, J. (2010) *Theory Construction and Model-Building Skills: A Practical Guide for Social Scientists*. New York: Guilford Press, p. 69.
3 Abraham, A. (2016) The imaginative mind, *Human Brain Mapping*, 37(11): 4197–4211.
4 National Advisory Committee on Creative and Cultural Education, *All Our Futures*.

They may have to undertake research or be taught elements of knowledge explicitly – camera angles and concepts like mise en scène, for example. But the knowledge alone is not enough – they are thinking about the relationship between the poet, film director and audience; they are applying imagination; they are making informed decisions, planning and creating. They are considering a number of interpretations and options. They are using skills and knowledge in tandem to create something new. They are taking one of the "best that has been thought and said" poets – who the traditionalists consider to be so important – and layering on top of their knowledge of the poet and his work skills and ideas which extend beyond the realms of the usual English literature classroom. Life doesn't exist in subjects and our attachment to organising knowledge into subject areas – rather than domains – limits us greatly.

Paul Howard-Jones' research into the neuroscientific evidence base for creativity suggests that being creative requires the brain to switch between generative and analytical activity.[5] There is, if you like, a mental switch between our imaginative ideas and our capacity to evaluate them and consider more logical processes. Furthermore, he points out that the teacher can create the conditions in which children can develop and "practice" their creativity, but that this requires switching between modes too. For example, in generative mode, lesson objectives can be restrictive, but in analytic mode they may be helpful. The stopover example offered here demands that the students switch between these hard and soft states – that they utilise a number of skills and attitudes in completing the tasks, all of which drives a deeper understanding and a connection to the poem. The children are forced to stand in the poem, not to look on from afar – a process that is both more meaningful and more memorable.

What is clear from the still relatively new field of neurological study into creativity is that – far from the idea that the brain has one creative side – in fact, the whole brain is involved during a creative process, switching from one mode of thinking to another depending on the task at hand.[6] Creative processes demand a flexibility of mind. Creativity is, in fact, a whole brain workout. To assume that by focusing on one kind of learning – the memorisation of knowledge – the capacity of the

---

5   Howard-Jones, P. (2008) *Fostering Creative Thinking: Co-constructed Insights from Neuroscience and Education.* Bristol: Higher Education Academy, Education Subject Centre.
6   Kaufman, S. (2013) The real neuroscience of creativity, *Scientific American* (19 August). Available at: https://blogs.scientificamerican.com/beautiful-minds/the-real-neuroscience-of-creativity/.

rest of the brain to spring into lateral, generative and critical thinking modes will engage "automatically" is woefully misguided. Children need to practise these modes of thinking by wading knee-deep in experiences that demand more of them than memorisation. That makes teaching more demanding. It also makes it infinitely more exciting.

chapter 3

The Graveyard

She felt the familiarity of the place, the warmth.

She was home.

What is dripping from the trees?

What words do the trees whisper?

What do the gravestones say?

Who tends to this graveyard?

Could this be a hopeful place?

If a statue should glance in our direction, what would we say and do?

The figure to the right looks into the graveyard. What is she looking for?

Your own questions ...

_____

_____

_____

_____

_____

_____

Download the image from www.crownhouse.co.uk/featured/uncharted-territories

The Graveyard

Graveyards provide rich contexts for learning, linking us to one of the key areas of philosophical inquiry – the matter of death. Whether it is through imagined contexts – such as ghost stories, for example, Neil Gaiman's *The Graveyard Book* – or through more practical considerations, we are forced to consider how we honour (or dishonour) and remember (or forget) those who have gone before us. The ideas in this section centre upon the idea of remembrance, but bring in the concept of responsibility and also practical considerations about how burial places are managed.

Primary Landmarks

⊙ **What if ...** you were a team of developers who have to relocate a graveyard after the sale of a church in order to make way for a new construction project? Where would it be relocated to? How would you remove the coffins and the gravestones and statues? Would you restore them or replace them? How should you lay out and organise the graveyard? How much room would each grave have? What facilities would there be for visitors? How would you ensure that it felt like a peaceful and pleasant place to be?

Concept: Remembrance and respect.

Lines of inquiry: Do human beings have the right to be treated respectfully after their death? Who owns human remains? To whom would we be accountable if we had to move remains to another burial site?

Curriculum areas: Laws and regulations about burial – formal writing and registers, sacred and secular burial sites – beliefs and values in religious and non-religious settings, measuring and planning to scale, designing, writing to inform and to present a particular point of view.

- **What if ...** you were a design team who have been asked to make a commemorative sculpture? After reading Susan Varley's *Badger's Parting Gifts* you could talk about how you would create a sculpture that would allow the animals to gather to remember and talk about Badger. If you lost a pet or someone you care about, how might you want to remember them? Why do people like to create memorials to people and things they don't want to forget, and how important is it to look after them? Can you think of other animals or characters from your favourite books or films who have died? What would their memorials be like?

  Concept: Loss.

  Lines of inquiry: How does remembering people help us to cope with losing them? Do memorials help us to remember important people?

  Curriculum areas: Coping with loss, emotive and memorial language, appropriateness of memorials, design, captioning, explanations.

- **What if ...** you discovered a tunnel leading to an underground labyrinth beneath the graveyard? What might be inside it? Who might live there? Where might other tunnels come out? You could link this idea with other images from this book – caves, forests, mountains, and so on. Could you design the labyrinth? If there are people or creatures living in it, what would their homes look like? If people are living under the ground, what do they do with their dead?

  Concept: Environments.

  Lines of inquiry: What demands would subterranean life place on human beings? What would you need in order to live underground? What would an underground home look like? What would life be like below ground? Do human beings need sunlight?

  Curriculum areas: Design, light and dark, imaginative and creative writing, problem solving – e.g. the challenges presented by subterranean life.

secondary landmarks

⊙ **What if ...** you were charged with the responsibility of managing a graveyard? Let's imagine that you work for a private company and the local authority has handed over the role of managing graveyards to your organisation. Would you control the kinds of words that can be written on a headstone or tomb, like some authorities have done? What kind of services would you offer? How much would you charge for tombstones, plaques, benches and other commemorative objects? Is there a fair price for grief and remembrance? Given that land is limited, would you encourage people to cremate rather than bury their loved ones? Would you cram graves in or leave space for mourners by the side? What would you do if you were asked to bury someone who had no money, family or friends and there would be no profit in it for you?

Concept: Capitalism and social responsibility.

Lines of inquiry: Is there a fair price for death? Is it right to make a profit from grief? Who has the right to say what is or is not appropriate for a memorial? Why might someone want to be buried in a private or secular graveyard instead of a church ground?

Curriculum areas: Law and governance, etiquette and tradition, beliefs and values, sustainability, land values and uses.

⊙ **What if ...** you were documentary makers asked to create a documentary about the ways in which human beings celebrate and commemorate death? What would you focus on? Why do we, as a society, fear the return of the dead when we miss our loved ones so much? Is this true of all cultures? What is the Día de los Muertos, celebrated mainly in Mexico and other Latino communities, about? How does it compare with Hallowe'en? How do funerals differ around the world? What are considered acceptable and unacceptable ways of mourning in different cultures?

Concept: Death.

Lines of inquiry: If death is an inevitable part of life, why do we fear it so much? How do other cultures deal with death?

Curriculum areas: Religion, beliefs, ethics, exploring cultural differences in approaches to talking about death.

◉ **What if ...** you were a team of scientists asked to create a series of animations or cartoons for children that explain what happens to people's bodies when they die? How could you include the correct scientific information and yet ensure your cartoons remain sensitive to the fact that the subject might upset or worry younger children?

Concept: Circle of life.

Lines of inquiry: How does death feed the earth? What is the circle of life? Do atoms die? Is it environmentally better to bury our dead?

Curriculum areas: Biological life cycles, atoms and physical processes, writing to inform and explain, sensitivity to audience.

◉ **What if ...** you were asked to create an informative text or a documentary about how the fallen are remembered in war? Using images of the D-Day war graves (see, for example, the American cemeteries at Omaha Beach and the smaller German cemeteries across Normandy), ask the group to consider how victory and defeat impact on the ways in which the dead are remembered. What examples of statues and monuments can they find?

Concept: Victory.

Lines of inquiry: How are victors and the defeated depicted? Is it true that history is written by the "winners"?

Curriculum areas: Symbols and icons, the creation of monuments as an historical source, writing with bias, writing for information.

◉ **What if ...** you were employed to do the "graveyard shift"? In Victorian times, people were employed to sit by the graves of the rich and listen out for the sound of a bell. The bell was placed inside the coffin in case the person was not dead after all and had in fact been buried alive. The "dead ringer" would pay to have the bell placed in their coffin. What if you heard the bell? What if you didn't?

Concept: Equality.

Lines of inquiry: Why were only rich people able to have this service? How could people have been buried alive in the first place? How come we no longer need this service?

Curriculum areas: Changing nature of work, inequality in Victorian times, ethics and economics, medical advances in technology.

a stopover

Originally devised for a Key Stage 3 social and cultural studies class, but could be applied to primary topic work, Key Stage 2 or 3 English classes or an integrated arts/humanities project.

Gather the class together informally and ask them the following questions:

"If we were a department in a local council that was responsible for the maintenance and upkeep of a cemetery, what kinds of values do you think we would have? What would we stand for?"

Discuss and write up a list of the things they think would be important regarding their roles and their values. Continue by saying, "What things would we not allow or never do?"

In groups, they can dramatise their prohibited action as a **still image** and caption it. Analyse the images and encourage other groups to look closely – "What do you notice about …? What might this gesture suggest?" You are encouraging a slow reading and deconstruction. Then ask:

"So how could we prevent these things from happening?"

They may suggest that you'll need:

- ⊙ Signage (e.g. do not walk on the graves, do not lean on the tombstones).

- ⊙ Security (CCTV or guards/police officers).

- ⊙ Rules (they will need to decide what these should be and how they will be communicated).

Then introduce a problem. A local newspaper has published a story with the head-line, "Dishonoured and Destroyed: The State of Our Town's Cemeteries". The article includes photographs of litter – beer bottles, fizzy drink cans, crisp packets and cigarette butts – strewn around the graves. There are also photographs of some tombstones pushed over and, in one case, a headstone with a symbol spray-painted on it – you might want to find real photographs to illustrate this, there are many available on the internet.

Get the students to draw these images onto a map of the cemetery to show where the problems are. What was the symbol? Whose headstone had been pushed over? Where was the litter? Where are the entrances and exits to the cemetery? What security is in place at the moment, other than the single CCTV camera at the main gate?

The CCTV camera is old and captures a single still image every ten seconds. It faces into the graveyard, but the angle is narrow and only a few graves and the main pathway are in shot – it certainly can't give us the full picture of what's happened. In groups, get the students to create a minute's worth of images from the day before – but make it clear that the camera has not actually captured the acts of vandalism. What did it capture? Given the camera's limited angle, what might have been happening out of shot? Who else was there? Were there other visitors who may have witnessed something?

Perhaps the CCTV did record a witness visiting one of the graves within the view of the camera. If so, could you identify who they are by the grave they visited? What might be on that tombstone to lead you to the witness? Once you've identified any witnesses, you could then **hot seat** them and ask what they saw – perhaps inviting them in for an interview. From the witnesses' descriptions, create identikits and descriptions of the suspects to be released to the public in an appeal for information.

You receive a phone call from someone who wishes to remain anonymous but who gives you the name of a local teenage boy. She is convinced he was there as the description you've released fits and she overheard him on the bus, bragging about "doing the graveyard in"! You can release this information to the class in a number of ways – by taking a "pretend" phone call or receiving an email or by prepping a child to tell the group, either in or out of role.

Assume the role of the boy and invite the class to interview you. Before they begin, get them to prepare their questions. Put in constraints – we want him to admit to it and to name the people he was with – so we might need to go in gently. We want him to talk, how will we draw him out if he is unwilling to do so? Given that the boy is under the age of 18, he will need to have an adult with him. Does one of the class want to take on the role of mum or dad? Alternatively you could assume this role and they could be the boy. Give the class some time to prepare their questions. While they do this, spend some time with the volunteer to plan a family backstory and brief them that the boy will eventually (but not straight away) admit what he did and name the other people involved. You can plan this together.

Fast-forwarding, the boy and the other culprits have eventually admitted what they did and instead of your security team reporting them to the police, you negotiate some community service which will allow them to tidy the cemetery and put right the damage. What jobs would you give them? What tools would they need?

Jumping forward again, after the boys have finished their community service, they report back to the group about issues they have noticed in the graveyard. You could explore this by giving information cards to members of the class or by reporting these findings to the class yourself using **teacher in role**. Their observations include:

- They've seen lots of older people coming in and having to stand for long periods of time by headstones. They noticed that there were few benches or places for them to sit down.
- They saw small children crying and refusing to come in because they said it was too scary.
- There were lots of dead flowers and there didn't seem to be a water source, so people couldn't fill up vases.
- There were lots of molehills.
- The paths were uneven and they saw several people trip up.
- Even the birds seemed to be silent. There were lots of weeds and brambles but few wild flowers. They felt it was a very depressing place to be.
- The gardeners contracted by the local authority came in to mow the lawns very quickly, but they didn't spend any time on other maintenance.

You could then go on to ask the class to come up with a redesign that would tackle these problems in addition to the original issue of security. Once the design work is completed they need to think about how to communicate what they have done and why. This could involve newspaper reports, press conferences or an event at the cemetery. They could gather statements from visitors to the remodelled cemetery. What do they think? How have things improved? Does the place feel different? The class could write these statements and read them out in role.

This work could lead the local council to commission a community film to remember those who went before us. This could include a gathering of voices and a collection of interviews – for example, interviews with relatives talking about memories of their loved ones and time spent with them in the local community – interspersed with images of the local area, both past and present, to create a living history project.

STEPPING STONES

You could:

- Create stories based on the words used on a gravestone.
- Use **role on the wall** to build up pictures of people based on their names and ages.
- Explore how the dead are treated differently in times of war, famine or peace.
- Do some research into how ancient civilisations – for example, the Egyptians or the Romans – treated their dead.
- Imagine you are responsible for the upkeep of a graveyard and are subject to relevant legislation – research what you are responsible for. Even though a graveyard may be long closed, the law says it must still be cared for. What has this old, forgotten graveyard seen? Graves which are over a hundred years old are recognised as having potential historical significance. Do communities have a responsibility for their graveyards other than through taxes?
- Investigate how graveyards and burial practices vary between religions.
- Visit a graveyard.

the bedrock – the importance of emotion

The view that emotion is a hindrance to reason has long persisted. The idea, stemming right back to Descartes' statement "I think, therefore I am", makes the assumption that rational decisions must be made without emotion. Also fundamental to Cartesian dualism is the idea that the mind and body are distinct entities. This binary view of thinking, and indeed of learning, persisted for centuries. In his book *Descartes' Error*, neuroscientist Antonio Damasio disproves the idea fairly conclusively.[1] In fact, all our decisions, unless we have a cognitive or psychological problem, come from an emotional place and these emotions are intrinsically connected to our bodies – they are "somatic". While emotion can override good sense, without it, we have psychopathy.

What's more, our emotions make for very deep memories and tapping into them can be a powerful tool in learning. Capturing the hearts of children – imbuing learning with emotive qualities – is deeply memorable. But of course these memories also need to link to content and to curriculum. It is not enough to scare or excite a child – the emotion needs to link to the experience and the knowledge that the lesson intended to convey. This is skilled work and demands a high level of questioning. Asking "How are we feeling at this moment?" along with "What do we know? What do we now need to consider?" is far more useful than simply asking "How do we feel?" The power is in the connections. Cognitive scientists Sidney D'Mello and Arthur Graesser point to the importance of "cognitive disequilibrium" in learning – the interruption of flow with something dissonant and unexpected.[2] It is at this point of interruption – the point of dilemma, we might say – that important emotional shifts in attention take place which greatly deepen learning and memory. Equilibrium can be "restored with thought, reflection and problem solving" in order to move the learning on, but if this processing is not done, learning can quickly turn to boredom and frustration. It is at the intersection between emotion and analysis that learning is most powerful. And, as we have learned, these are also the key components of creative thinking.

....

1 Damasio, A. (1995) *Descartes' Error: Emotion, Reason and the Human Brain*. New York: Putnam.
2 D'Mello, S. and Graesser, A. (2012) Dynamics of affective states during complex learning, *Learning and Instruction*, 22(2): 145–157.

This intersection is even more fundamental for the adolescent brain. Cognitive neuroscientist Sarah-Jayne Blakemore's work on the ways in which teenagers' brains change during adolescence offers us some insight into how emotions, self-regulation and risk taking are all affected by hormones.[3] Teenagers' limbic brains, associated with emotion, are in overdrive. Working through and managing that emotion – for example, by practising self-regulation through tackling dilemmas – can help to stimulate learning and help make teenagers feel safe and in control of situations.

It's important that we attend to this complexity because, as psychologist Marc Smith points out, learning is not simply a cognitive process. It is not a matter of residual memory – a view that persists in some areas of the educational establishment. In fact, according to Smith, learning sits at the heart of a complex relationship between cognitive, emotional and social processes.[4] What many of the examples in this book attempt to do, therefore, is to bring these three realms of learning together into a "practised environment" – that is an environment in which problems, pressures, predicaments and possibilities can be practised. It brings fictional goals into view – goals that can be explored now and that don't rely on a future test to act as an external motivational force.

The power of dilemma and the power of story then, sit at the heart of what we do as educators because they sit at the heart of deep learning for children. The skilled teacher will choreograph the dance between flow, confusion, resolve and reflection, all within an emotional frame. This is putting teaching to work rather than simply following a script. And it makes being in the classroom a joyful affair for both teacher and student, even as they grapple with difficulty.

....

3 Blakemore, S-J. (2012) The mysterious workings of the teenage brain, *Ted.com* [video]. Available at: https://www.ted.com/talks/sarah_jayne_blakemore_the_mysterious_workings_of_the_adolescent_brain.

4 Smith, M. (2018) *The Emotional Learner: Understanding Emotions, Learners and Achievement*. Abingdon: Routledge, p. 7.

chapter 1
the mountain

Obstacles littered the path, not least the darkness.

And so, it began.

What lies at the base of the mountain?

What figures can be seen? Are they "real"?

Who carved these figures for us to find and why?

There appears to be an opening at the base of the mountain. Who created it? Where does it go?

What lies underneath the mountain? Is it a mine?

What do they mine? Who are they?

Could we find this mountain on a map? What sort of map?

Your own questions ...

_____

_____

_____

_____

Download the image from www.crownhouse.co.uk/featured/uncharted-territories

the mountain

Mountains are riddled with stories. They represent the ancient, the unobtainable and the unknown. They are found in classic works of literature as well as in contemporary accounts of human endeavour. They can remind us to think about the natural world and humanity's place within it. They can also be a reminder of the fragility of our lives and of our struggle for survival. They represent a sense of time that goes way beyond our narrow human concept of it – set against the vastness of geological time, human lives seem small and insignificant. Learning about mountains can help children to understand scale as well as consider deeper philosophical ideas about our place on this planet.

primary landmarks

- **What if …** you were asked to help the Mountain King, who is worried that all the people who are trying to climb his mountain will spoil it? He is also worried that they might one day find his magical fairy kingdom, hidden deep in the mountain, and capture him and his subjects. How can you help him and his people to preserve and protect his sacred mountain? What if, one day, a child stumbled in there by mistake?

  Concept: Protection.

  Lines of inquiry: How far might you go to protect your home from others? Should some places be left alone?

  Curriculum areas: Fairy tales and related stories – leading to creative and descriptive writing, exploration of erosion and impact of tourism, geological time versus human time, the life of mountains, scale and significance.

- **What if …** you were a team of vets at an animal rescue centre? What kinds of tasks might you have to do? Who else works in your centre? What if one day, someone brought in an injured golden eagle? How big is a golden eagle?

What do they look like? Are they safe to handle? This eagle seems to have a broken wing – there is a hole in it – it seems to have been shot. How do you fix a bird's broken wing? How will you take care of it until you can return it to the wild? Where is its nest? And does it have eaglets that need care and protection? How will you find them and care for them? What will you do about the hunting and shooting that takes place on the land at the side of the mountain? Can you protect other birds from this fate?

Concept: Conservation and protest.

Lines of inquiry: How can we protect the natural world? How do we harm it? How do we care for creatures that might harm us? How do we prevent people from harming animals?

Curriculum areas: Geographical mapping, problem solving, animal habitats and care, writing to inform and persuade.

◉ **What if …** you were asked to design a snowy playground for an alpine village? What kinds of things would be fun to play on in the snow? The villagers want something that will keep children fit, be good fun and educate them about staying safe in the snow. You might even have an igloo building area! How would you ensure your playground was safe and yet allowed children to explore and have fun?

Concept: Play.

Lines of inquiry: What is the value of play? Why do human beings like to be entertained? Do people grow out of needing or liking to play?

Curriculum areas: Freezing and melting, healthy bodies, building structures that will stay up, keeping safe, properties of snow.

secondary landmarks

◉ **What if …** you were a government department responsible for environmental protection in the mountain region? There is a remote village on the far side of the mountain. For years the people living there have struggled to make the terrible journey around the side of the mountain to gain access to medical support and other services and supplies. The villagers have tried to convince the government to build an access tunnel going through the mountain, reducing their journey time to the town by fourteen hours. You have to make the decision as the village falls under your jurisdiction. Can you balance the clear needs of the villagers with the wider community expectations around landscape preservation? Having considered all these issues, will you go ahead? If so, how will it be done? What do the drilling machines look like? How would you get these big machines to where they need to be? How would you ensure everyone working on the project – mechanics, engineers and geologists – and local residents are kept safe? What's the timeline of such a project? How will the official opening be celebrated? If you decide not to build the tunnel, how will you explain your decision to the villagers?

Concept: Progress versus protection.

Lines of inquiry: Is it right to change the landscape for our convenience? What are the dangers of tunnelling? Does convenience come at a cost? How do people protest?

Curriculum areas: Practical considerations – applied uses of STEM subjects, environmental geography, design and technology, ethics of conservation, discussions and debates, writing to persuade and inform.

⊙ **What if …** we were invited to ascend Mount Everest as part of a larger international expedition? Our role is to collect stories of the mountain and to research the history of those who have climbed it in the past. What if we find that the mountain is not simply a place for stories of success, but also a mass graveyard? What if we were commissioned to commemorate the dead, long since buried in the ice? What would we do? Could we take them home? How? If we leave them there, how would we remember them?

Concept: Human endeavour.

Lines of inquiry: Are people who take risks with their lives heroes or fools? Who should foot the bill for the recovery of people, injured or deceased, who take such risks?

Curriculum areas: Forces and the impact of falls, human biology and the supply of oxygen at altitude, weather conditions on mountains, geology, impact of mountains on gravity as they form and vice versa, reporting and recording, remembrance and ethics, transportation and costs.

⊙ **What if** ... you were responsible for well-being, fitness and safety at a mountain sports retreat? Mountain sports have become increasingly popular over recent years, with many amateurs taking to the hills to try snowboarding, skiing, climbing and trail running. You will be offering an introductory programme at the retreat that will take the form of a taster weekend. Design an itinerary that will measure delegates' starting fitness levels, offer taster experiences to inspire them, provide healthy food options and sample fitness programmes to take away. It's important that the weekend itinerary offers a healthy and inspirational experience. You will need to brand the weekend and think about how you will get your information out to the people you hope to attract.

Concept: Health.

Lines of inquiry: How do our bodies and minds stay healthy? How can we encourage people to enjoy physical activity and health? Is it right to profit from people's concerns about their health?

Curriculum areas: Human biology and health, PSHE, business and marketing.

a stopover

This would be well-suited to geography, drama or English lessons with 11–14-year-olds, and would also be suitable for primary topic work.

Show the children an image of a large volcanic mountain. Villarrica in Chile is a great example as it's clearly surrounded by human settlements. There are around 1,500 active volcanoes in the world, with an estimated 800 million people living on or near them.[1] Discuss why people would choose to live close to an active volcano.

What do the children already know about volcanoes? Gather their information and, together, draw a diagram of the cross section of a volcano. Guide them towards reliable sources of knowledge if they are making assumptions or mistakes.

1 See https://news.nationalgeographic.com/2015/04/150410-tambora-volcano-eruption-climate-change-famine-earth-science/.

Look at the diagram and ask the children to mark the site of a village either on the side or at the foot of the mountain. Begin to explore and question:

"Let's map our village. How many houses are there? Anything else? Is there a school? A medical centre? Shops? Roads? How many? Where do they lead to? Let's add in one road – it ends at the gate to the place where many of the local people work. It is a mineral mine. What is a mine? What kinds of jobs might people do here?"

The children could perform these jobs as an **occupational mime** and do some research into what a mine looks like, the kinds of minerals a volcano might provide and the uses of those minerals.

Get the children to research and prepare a short information leaflet about what to do in the event of a volcanic eruption. Give them the opening sentence:

"If scientists and government officials think that the volcano is showing signs of erupting, a warning siren will be sounded and the evacuation procedure will begin. You should …"

Get the children to list their advice about what to do in the event of an eruption. What other information does the leaflet need to contain in order to be most helpful? They could include:

- An explanation of what a volcano is, with a diagram.
- Key words such as molten rock, magma and lahar.
- An emphasis on how dangerous an eruption could be and the importance of responding quickly.
- Guidance on being ready to leave at a moment's notice.

Once the leaflets are finished, ask the children to think about the idea of having to leave home quickly. Would they keep a bag packed by the door ready for emergencies? What would be in it? Continue to question:

"Let's look again at our map and at the road out of the village. Consider how many people and cars there are in the village. Would it be possible to get away quickly? How much warning do volcanoes give when they are about to erupt? What are the warning stages? Currently the village is on a code 3 alert which means that the volcano is highly active and expected to erupt at some point in the not too distant future. This could be a matter of months or years, but it is fairly inevitable. What is it like to live with this kind of warning?"

You could explore the views of different people who live in the village. What do they think and feel about the volcano? You could deliver the statements using **teacher in role**, or ask the children to step into character. Possible characters to explore could include:

- A scientist who is living there to monitor the situation.
- The owner of the mine.
- A mother with a small baby.
- A disabled, elderly person who is living alone.
- The owner of the local grocery store.
- A child.
- A journalist hoping for an exclusive scoop on the eruption.
- The government official who would oversee the evacuation should it happen.
- A man who has lived there all his life and is determined not to move.

Start the next lesson as if it is a general public meeting, assuming the role of a police officer. Announce to the children that there is now a code 4 alert in place – eruption is imminent. It could happen any time in the next 24 hours, or in the next few days. A full-scale evacuation of the village has been ordered. But there is a problem – only one bus has been sent. People will need to be evacuated one bus load at a time. Who needs to go first?

The class are then asked to be the evacuation committee – it will be their job to go house to house and check that everyone has left. They will be the last to leave. How do they feel about this? If they could only send one text to their families, what would it say? Staying in role, ask the evacuation committee to plan what they would do if faced with the following scenarios:

- They may find that the local farmers refuse to leave their animals behind. Consider what is to be done with family pets, livestock and animals. Are they a priority?

- They may have to persuade a resident who is reluctant to leave. What might the arguments be for staying, or for forcing someone to leave against their wishes?

- They have to decide who will travel on the first bus and why.

- They may catch a colleague stealing from an abandoned house. The colleague shrugs and says, "It would have been destroyed anyway. What's the harm?" What would they do?

- As they leave, they take some final photographs before the village is destroyed. What do they choose to photograph and why?

- They may have to deal with the journalist who insists on following them to document the evacuation. How might this complicate matters? What might the journalist write?

- Before they have finished the evacuation procedure, they are ordered to leave – there is no more time. However, there are still some people left in the village – what should they do?

- In the days after the volcano erupts they read about what happened in the papers. What might be written about the evacuation? How might their actions and decisions be written about next week? Next year? How might the media judge them? Might this change over time? If they had to reflect back later, do they think they'd still be happy with the decisions they made?

STEPPING STONES

You could:

- Research how old some mountain ranges are. Do mountains change shape over time?

- Research glacial formation and movement. What is happening to glaciers on mountains? What impact is climate change having on mountains and on the habitats of animals?

- Create infographics explaining how mountains are formed to help others understand this process.

- Pack for a trip up a mountain. What will you need to take with you? Will it get hotter or colder as you get closer to the sun?

- Explore how sound travels in valleys and on mountain tops. What is an echo? If you got into difficulty and needed to call for help, where would be the best places to stand in order to be heard or seen?

- Research avalanches and what you should do in order to survive one.

- Visit a mountain.

THE BEDROCK – ORACY

Fairly high up on the list of effective interventions in the EEF's toolkit is "collaborative learning" with a gain of +5 months' progress.[2] Yet many people find group work difficult to manage and so seek to undermine its importance by focusing on other strategies (self-quizzing, for example). The fact is that human beings are social animals. We know that even just telling a child they will need to teach someone else what they have learned improves retention.[3] But we need to know more about why this way of working can be effective, and how best to manage it.

....

2 See https://educationendowmentfoundation.org.uk/evidence-summaries/teaching-learning-toolkit/collaborative-learning/.
3 Brown, P. C. et al. (2014) *Make It Stick: The Science of Successful Learning*. Cambridge, MA: Belknap Press.

One of the key components of collaborative learning is talk. Talk can shape the mind.[4] It also builds vocabulary and fosters empathy. For these reasons alone, talk matters in the classroom. Sarah Michaels and colleagues' research into accountable talk outlines three key conditions for purposeful, mind building talk: it must be (1) accountable to the group – everyone plays a part, (2) accountable to knowledge – the talk is well informed and supporting facts are researched and presented, and (3) accountable to reason – talk is purposefully constructed and presented with a clear aim.[5] In order to be accountable in these areas, children need vocabulary, confidence and the capacity to organise their thoughts. When accountable talk is placed in a dilemma-led context, exciting things happen. This kind of talk is purposeful and dialogic – teachers do not have all the answers. They probe for deeper understanding, make the children reach for solutions and question inductively. When dialogic talk is established in class, outcomes for children are shown to improve not only in English, which one might expect, but also in maths and science.[6]

Children, when given the role of persuading residents who are reluctant to do so to leave their homes, are accountable in all three areas. But the urgency of the context also places them in a realm in which emotion and empathy are working in conjunction. For us, dramatic contexts offer a unique starting point in which speech, action, imagination, knowledge, problem solving, urgency, empathy and emotion are brought together. This is a potent mix for building purpose. Finding those moments in which the children work together for a common good – be that in a fictional or real context – is gold dust for the teacher. Drama offers limitless possibilities.

Talk in the classroom is, of course, not always about being in role. It's about being informed, making decisions, identifying problems and solving them. It's about communicating the information you need to pass on as effectively as possible. It's about understanding that talk is as much about sound and gesture as it is about words. It needs to be practised – by adults as much as by children.

....

4 Mercer, N. (2000) *Words and Minds: How We Use Language to Think Together.* Abingdon: Routledge.
5 Michaels, S. et al. (2008) Deliberative discourse idealized and realized: accountable talk in the classroom and in civic life, *Studies in Philosophy and Education*, 27(4): 283.
6 Jay, T. et al. (2017) *Dialogic Teaching: Evaluation Report and Executive Summary.* London: Education Endowment Foundation. Available at: https://educationendowmentfoundation.org.uk/public/files/Projects/Evaluation_Reports/Dialogic_Teaching_Evaluation_Report.pdf.

Being inarticulate – being unable to put across your point of view – is one of the most frustrating experiences a human being can have. To be inarticulate is to leave yourself open to put-down, belittlement, misunderstanding and misconception. It is to find yourself silenced. It is to be cut off. And while psychologist Jerome Bruner reminds us of the fact that we can often meet the "inarticulate genius" and the "articulate idiot", the truth is that in our society the latter is better rewarded.[7] Arming children with language, while recognising the importance of prelinguistic gesture, is vital if we are to build their confidence in speech. Children will often gesture conceptual knowledge before they can speak it, and teachers who gesture well are more likely to be understood.[8] In fact, studies show that developing gesture in children leads to better verbal articulacy too.[9]

This is why woven into all of these ideas are moments in which children create images, gestures and movements, communicating meaning which can then be analysed. It is why the work is infused with talk, with questions, with problems and with difficulties. It is why we have woven the linguistic, symbolic and physical together – to build articulate communities of learning, who work together towards a common understanding.

7   Bruner, J. (1976) *The Process of Education*. Cambridge, MA: Harvard University Press.

8   Goldin-Meadow, S. and Wagner, S. M. (2005) How our hands help us learn, *Trends in Cognitive Sciences*, 9(5): 234–241.

9   Demir, Ö. E. et al. (2014) A tale of two hands: children's early gesture use in narrative production predicts later narrative structure in speech, *Journal of Child Language*, 42: 662–681.

the ship

"It's the stories from the long dead sailors that we should fear the most," she whispered. Her father simply looked on into the distance.

What constitutes "a life on the ocean wave"?

Who is the nautical figurehead on this ship?

Who carved the figurehead?

What could the figurehead tell us of the ship's voyages?

Who are the figures on the shoreline?

Are they bidding farewell or waiting for news?

An ocean of books? What tales could they tell?

Your own questions ...

_____

_____

_____

_____

_____

_____

_____

Download the image from www.crownhouse.co.uk/featured/uncharted-territories

the ship

For island nations, the sea plays a huge part in the development of their culture and their traditional stories. From pirates to sea battles, ghost ships to smugglers, coastlines are littered with seafaring stories. Ships can represent both safety and danger, adventure and entrapment. From being ice locked to speeding across the ocean, from being storm ravaged to becalmed and adrift, ships captivate our imaginations from an early age.

primary landmarks

⊚ **What if ...** while reading Oliver Jeffers' *Lost and Found* you decide to help the boy and the penguin? Before they launch the boat, what will you advise them to pack in their small suitcase? What might the weather be like on the journey and at the South Pole? What other countries might they visit along the way? Could you help them to explore the stories, songs, food and languages of those countries? What would the boy write in postcards home? Could you write them for him? What does a storm sound like? What is it like to be in the middle of the ocean and not be able to see the sky? What stories would he tell the penguin? When they arrive home, what other adventures might they have?

Concept: Friendship and loneliness.

Lines of inquiry: What if you realised your new companion was not lost but just lonely? What is loneliness? How would you entertain someone else on a long journey?

Curriculum areas: Languages, geography, climate, phonics (making the sounds of the sea and storms and turning them into phonic poems), cultures, food, rituals and beliefs, hot and cold, floating and sinking, marine wildlife.

◉ **What if ...** you were asked to prepare for a voyage to an uninhabited island? Your ship is very modern and has everything you need for a safe trip. What would you need for a safe journey? What messages would you write for the people left behind? What would the photographs of the ship's launch look like? Who appears in them? Is the launch a happy or sad event? What questions do people ask the explorers before they leave? What are the explorers really thinking? Are you excited or worried about the trip? How long do you think you will be at sea? What do you hope to find on the island?

Concept: Adventure.

Lines of inquiry: Is it ever possible to have risk free adventure? If an island is uninhabited, does that mean nothing lives there?

Curriculum areas: Human settlements, establishing culture and laws, hierarchies and democracies, resourcefulness, making use of natural resources, how to find food, shelter and safe drinking water.

◉ **What if ...** there were rumours of an old ghost ship roaming along the edge of the coastline near your village? The ship is only seen on nights where there is a new moon, when light is low. Witnesses say that the ship is crewed by ghostly figures and that where it touches the water, the waves transform into the pages of books. The characters in them sound out over the splashing of the water – wailing and crying, laughter and joy, breathing and sighing, yelling and singing ... the sounds of stories and songs. What tales does the ghostly ship tell? Why does it appear and who are its ghosts?

Concept: Secrets.

Lines of inquiry: Why are ghost stories still so popular in our culture? How does the past echo through time? If people from the past could speak with us, what would they say?

Curriculum areas: The history of an island nation, the role ships have played in our past, literary texts featuring ghosts or ships (e.g. "The Rime of the Ancient Mariner" by Samuel Taylor Coleridge), literary genre, writing to describe and entertain.

secondary landmarks

- **What if ...** you were to compare the sinking of the *Titanic* with the sinking of the *Costa Concordia*? To what extent were both incidents an example of the folly of human arrogance and conceit? Can we ever be truly safe when we travel or should we accept that we take our lives in our hands whenever we step inside a vessel that will be sent into the sky or out onto the ocean? What if you worked for a travel company who wanted to create an adventure experience to show people what it is really like to take your life into your hands at sea? What if your company recreated an 18th century sailing vessel and offered crew places as part of a gap year experience? How much responsibility would you have for your clients? What kinds of experiences would be built in? How would you market the experience and what would your contracts and disclaimers say? Where would you go? If disaster struck, how would you respond?

  Concept: Human arrogance.

  Lines of inquiry: Is our own arrogance the biggest threat to our species? Would you trust a machine more than a human being to sail a ship, drive a car or fly a plane?

  Curriculum areas: Design, marketing, product safety, law, ethics, writing to persuade and inform.

- **What if ...** you were innovators in ship design? You are researching the creation of low-cost vessels powered with renewable energies that can be used in emergencies or for recreation. From what could these vessels be made? How could they be powered? How much would they cost? What benefits would your ship design bring to attempts to tackle climate change? What might be the problems with your design?

  Concept: Responsible innovation.

  Lines of inquiry: What are the barriers to getting rid of boats and ships powered by fossil fuels? Does short-term profit trump long-term survival?

  Curriculum areas: Design, renewable energies, cost–benefit analysis, properties of materials, climate change and energy consumption.

◉ **What if ...** you worked on a luxury yacht – *The King of the Waves* – and your clients were all very wealthy? What jobs might you do? Are you proud of the yacht? How do you interact with the passengers? Could you create images of a day in the life of the workers and passengers on the yacht? How would a holiday on this yacht be advertised? Could you plan the itinerary of a Mediterranean cruise on this yacht? Choose a point in the journey between two destinations and imagine you are looking out to sea. You see another boat on the horizon. Now flip the story. What if ... you were desperate to leave your country and had to cross the sea to reach another land? What if you had your children with you? If you had to flee in a hurry, what would you take with you? If you were asked to pay for passage across the sea, what precautions would you take? How would you keep your family safe? What would you say to your partner to persuade them to leave and take this chance? Back to the yacht ... you are standing on deck enjoying the view when you see another boat crossing the sea. It is crowded. It seems to be sinking. What is the name of that boat? People are screaming and waving at you. What do you do?

Concept: Refugees.

Lines of inquiry: Will self-interest always win the day? Do people have a right to a safe home? What lengths would you go to to save your family and give them the hope of a better life?

Curriculum areas: The refugee crisis, the geography of the Middle East and Europe, population movement and migration, human rights, the role of the United Nations High Commissioner for Refugees (UNHCR), life in refugee camps.

a stopover

This scenario was originally delivered in a primary school but would be equally suitable for Key Stage 3. It explores life in a different time and how things have changed.

Arrange battery powered tea lights in lanterns around the room – these are safer than real candles. If possible, dull the lights in the classroom. As the children enter, they are told that the year is 1878.

Sit and discuss: if the year is 1878, what is different about our daily lives? For example, what technology are we living without? This helps the children find a sense of time. What if we lived in a village by the sea? What jobs would we be doing in 1878? Perhaps pause to do some research into 19th century fishing communities.

In groups, ask the children to create **still images** of the different workers: the fishermen, the landlord, the butcher, the teacher, the beachcombers, the line-baiters, the barrel-makers, the basket-weavers, the farmers and the skippers. **Thought track** these still images to explore what the workers think about their lives. How do their gestures communicate whether or not they like their work? Whether or not it is too difficult? How important it is to their survival? Reflect further upon what life is like in the community. Women barter with local farmers to exchange fish for vegetables. Life is given by the land and the sea. Is this still true today?

Ask the children to think about who is in charge of decisions in the village. Do some people have more power than others? Do some people have more wealth? Think about the houses in which the workers live. More than likely these will be small, single room dwellings. These buildings would be owned by a landlord – let's say he is a local landowner and farmer – rather than by the occupants.

What would a floor plan of one of those cottages look like? Could the children either draw their own or mark one up with sticky notes? You could create the out-line on the floor with masking tape so they can label the rooms. Discuss how many people live there and what the daily routine is.

Then, a note is circulated around the people of the village:

Assemble at the church at 6 p.m.

– by order of the landlord

A note like this worries the villagers – they fear the landlord might be putting rents up.

Having created still images of the workers, let's now still image the people waiting in the church for the landlord. How can the feeling of uncertainty be conveyed? Thought track the villagers' fears and feelings.

Who is this landlord? What does he look like? What does he think of the villagers? You could begin a **role on the wall** and add to it after the class has heard what he has to say.

As teacher you can take on the role of the landlord. Remember, this isn't acting, it's presenting the information the children need to move the activity on. We usually preface a shift to being in role with the words, "I'll speak as …"

The landlord says:

"I see you have your lanterns. Good. You'll be needing them if you know what's good for you. The world's getting more expensive and prices are going up. And we can't all live on fish. Now then, my friend owns a ship that's going to be passing by our bay later tonight. The ship and its men are worthless but the cargo will be worth something. If the boat is wrecked, my friend can claim on the shipping insurance. I don't expect you to understand all that – I just need you on those cliffs tonight, luring that ship onto the rocks."

Ask the children what we have heard from the landlord. What is he asking us to do? Who will benefit from his request? Gather their immediate reactions to the landlord onto sticky notes and place these around the role on the wall. Amend the role on the wall in light of what we now know. Weigh up the decision the class now needs to make:

"Are we going to do as the landlord asks? How will we benefit? Is he threatening us? Is it okay to stand by and let the ship and its crew flounder? What about the risk to human life? Wrecking is illegal and a hangable offence, are we comfortable with taking the risk to save our livelihoods?"

In groups, the children can weigh up their thoughts and present back.

Still holding our lanterns, we now stand on the cliff edge. The ship will be passing soon, but what are we going to do? Divide the class into two groups. Ask group A to offer reasons for going through with the landlord's wishes, while group B can argue against. Present these at the cliff edge.

This might be a good place to pause the session for further reflection and exploration. You could write diary entries as the villagers or script a conversation between them for a literacy outcome.

In terms of where to go next, there are a number of opportunities. The hope is that the children are steered towards going against the landlord's demands, but this is something that should be worked towards and not just with teacher-led direction.

Additional scenarios to explore could include:

⊙ Changing the role of the children so they become the crew of the potentially doomed ship. Create a class still image of the crew seeing the lights on the cliff. The landlord's plot could fail if the crew are wary of the lanterns. There are more opportunities here for thought tracking and dialogue.

⊙ A number of the villagers go to the landlord to appeal to him to change his mind about wrecking the ship. How might he react? What should the villagers say? How should they deliver what they want to say?

⊙ It is now 24 hours after the event. The ship is wrecked, the cargo is ashore and the villagers are rescuing sailors in fishing boats. With masking tape, create the outline of a boat and sit a number of children inside with the rest of the class sat around the outside. What questions do the class have for the occupants of the boat? How do the villagers and crew in the boat feel towards each other? Do the crew need to know the truth? Is it ever okay to lie? There is a reward for saving sailors from shipwrecks – who will keep that reward? Is it right to do so?

⊙ The class are in role as modern historians looking back at the events of that night. Can they retell the story using images and text to create informative display boards for visitors to the area?

⊙ A local author decides to turn the tale into a ghost story about a mysterious ship that haunts the coastline near the village. How might that story be told? Who are the villains? Are there any heroes? How is the story illustrated?

stepping stones

You could:

- Prepare the inventory of the ship and compare it with a modern-day inventory.

- Look at the geography of ship manufacture – how has it altered in the last century?

- Describe the sinking of a ship and the rescue of its crew from the point of view of two witnesses – a journalist and the ship's owner.

- Map out the various floors of a modern cruise ship. What rooms does it have? Where are the escape routes?

- Create a ticket price list for people wishing to journey from Liverpool to America in the 19th century.

- Write accounts for passengers on a voyage across the Atlantic.

- Make a boat from discarded plastic and rubbish. Can you test its seaworthiness?

- Plot a cruise that will show passengers four contrasting cultures.

- Design a lifeboat station.

- Organise a protest against the closure of a lifeboat station.

- Read poems describing life on the waves, create soundscapes and compose music that evokes life at sea.

- Listen to sea shanties and write your own.

- Visit a ship.

The bedrock – empathy

Many of the ideas in this book are rooted in the concept of playful, imaginative endeavour and so far we have looked at the importance of play, imagination, talk, gesture, emotion and story. All of these are necessary if children are to develop empathy. Empathy is critical to the security and safety of all human beings. The mission statement of the IB includes the aim that children will "understand that other people, with their differences, can also be right".[1] Think about that statement. How would it affect our world if this were indeed the case? Of course this isn't to insist that other people are always right, but that they can be. Such understanding is critical to building a better world and that starts with empathy.

Empathy is not the same as compassion, but it is an element of compassion. It is possible to empathise with how someone feels, but not to act in order to alleviate their suffering. A compassionate person wants to act. If we truly want children to grow into wise adults who act to build a better world, then empathy is a good place to start. But this needs to be part of a bigger picture that ensures compassion, action and service – skills that are vital for a successful adult life. These skills matter if we want children to be able to cope with uncertainty and complexity.

According to endurance athlete and coach Christopher Bergland, "Because our brain's neural circuitry is malleable and can be rewired through neuroplasticity one's tendency for empathy and compassion is never fixed. We all need to practice putting ourselves in someone else's shoes to reinforce the neural networks that allow us to 'love thy neighbor as thyself'."[2] It would seem to us that practising multiple perspectives in role is one way in which these neural pathways can be formed and reinforced. Normal classroom interactions don't offer enough opportunity for children to really place themselves in the shoes of others; to speak their words, act out their behaviours and gestures, think their thoughts – but they should. Working in this manner is not simply a way of making children more imaginative or creative, nor is it about fun. It's about placing them in an empathy gym in which they have to work out how to respond and react. And this way of working seems to impact, according to psychologist E. Glenn Schellenberg, on children's prosocial behaviours. Schellenberg found that the drama group he used as a control when researching the impact of music on IQ improved their social skills by 72%.[3]

....

1 See http://www.ibo.org/about-the-ib/mission/.
2 Bergland, C. (2013) The Neuroscience of Empathy, *Psychology Today* (10 October). Available at: https://www.psychologytoday.com/blog/the-athletes-way/201310/the-neuroscience-empathy.
3 Schellenberg, G. E. (2004) Music lessons enhance IQ, *Psychological Science*, 15(8): 511–514. Available at: https://doi.org/10.1111/j.0956-7976.2004.00711.x, at p. 513.

A study undertaken at the Max Planck Institute for Human Cognitive and Brain Sciences reinforces the idea that empathy can be learned and practised, but also shows that people best demonstrate the quality when there is time to think and when they are not under undue stress.[4] Creating learning spaces for children which mean they have time to engage with dilemma, to think through how situations impact on others and in which they themselves feel safe, comfortable and secure, is vital in order to create the conditions in which empathy can thrive. Too little attention is paid in our planning to the development of this critical human trait and, too often, under stress and time pressure ourselves, teachers create exactly the learning conditions that will suppress the development of children's empathy – making them more ego driven and selfish.

When we make decisions about curriculum and learning, we have to be clear about our long-term goals. What do we want for the future of our planet and for the people living on it? How can education help us to achieve those aims? Are we better off with well-qualified people or with wise people? Are the two mutually exclusive? Thinking about the answers to these questions should help us to form mission statements and value systems for our schools that have these longer term aims in mind. This means looking beyond test results – seeing them almost as a by-product of a good education rather than the end product. If we truly look at what we want for the future, beyond the school leaving age, we would surely put compassion and empathy near to the top of our list of the desirable outcomes of education. And to achieve this we need to place children in as many situations as possible in which they need to use their imagination, knowledge and empathy to solve unpredictable problems and dilemmas.

What is emerging as the disparate areas of research are brought together is that emotion, empathy, embodied cognition, narrative, imagination and play combine to make for powerful learning experiences. That in itself is a wonderful thing. But when you consider the impact that an emotionally intelligent, empathetic, healthy, imaginative person can have on the world, we start to see the true purpose of education emerging, and a better world too. There's nothing wrong with aiming high!

....

4   Singer, T. (2015) How to build a caring economy, *World Economic Forum* (24 January). Available at: https://www.weforum.org/agenda/2015/01/how-to-build-a-caring-economy/.

Chapter 6

The universe

We look up to the heavens and everything is laid out before us.

Who looks back into our collective scrutiny?

Who is the woman?

How is the universe reflected in her face?

What is she thinking?

What does she see in the stars?

Is that a man in the moon?

Are the sun and the moon opposites?

Your own questions ...

Download the image from www.crownhouse.co.uk/featured/uncharted-territories

The universe

We challenge you to show us a child who isn't interested in space – the vastness, the possibilities, the unknowns. Space is still the final frontier (unless, of course, we do find that parallel universes exist, in which case there are infinite frontiers). Are there aliens out there? Does our smallness in the vast expanse of space make us more or less significant? Astrophysicist Carl Sagan, in his book *Pale Blue Dot*, reflects on the image of earth taken from the edges of the solar system, in which it appears as a speck of dust in a beam of light. He contemplates the energy expended on this "barely distinguishable pixel" in battles for power and supremacy and concludes that, "There is perhaps no better demonstration of the folly of human conceit than this distant image of our tiny world. To me, it underscores our responsibility to deal more kindly with one another, and to preserve and cherish the pale blue dot, the only home we've ever known."[1]

In this chapter, we too explore our place in the universe and on our own planet, in both real and imagined contexts.

primary landmarks

⊙ **What if …** you came into school one day to find odd footprints on the walls and ceilings? There is a slimy substance in the sink. On the floor is an ID card, with the words "intergalactic peace force" written across the top. The photo on the ID card is like no creature you've ever seen before. What is this alien's name? How would you help the alien to get home? Would you have to report them to the authorities?

Concept: Helping others.

....

1 Sagan, C. (1994) *Pale Blue Dot: A Vision of the Human Future in Space*. New York: Random House. Quoted extract available at: http://www.planetary.org/explore/space-topics/earth/pale-blue-dot. html.

Lines of inquiry: How do we know if we can trust someone? Is it ever right to keep secrets from the authorities? What is a peace force? What human customs and habits might the alien find odd? How would we explain our lives to them?

Curriculum areas: Key language of space – planets, moons, galaxies and the universe, creative writing, role play.

⊙ **What if …** after reading *How to Catch a Star* by Oliver Jeffers, you decide to teach the little boy in the story about real stars and about why he can't catch one? Why does he want a star so much? Do you think he is lonely? Could you befriend him and show him how exciting space is? Could you create your own book all about the planets and stars?

Concept: Loneliness.

Lines of inquiry: Why might someone not have friends? How can we help someone who is lonely? What are stars made of?

Curriculum areas: Light and reflection, stars and space, shapes, friendships.

⊙ **What if …** you could discover stories in the stars? Find out about the story of Andromeda. Who was she? How was she rescued? Do the stars link us to people in the past? Who named the galaxies and why? What are the stories behind the names of the stars, galaxies and planets?

Concept: Making meaning.

Lines of inquiry: Before space travel was possible and before telescopes were invented, how did people make sense of the sky? How did their beliefs and experiences impact on their view of space and of their place in the universe? Do stories reflect our attempts to understand the unknown?

Curriculum areas: Myths and legends linked to the sky and space, religions and beliefs, the role of science in developing human understanding, astronomy versus astrology.

secondary landmarks

⦿ **What if ...** after reading Carl Sagan's *Pale Blue Dot*, you explore the link between science and religion?[2] Sagan makes us think about human behaviour and our place in the world. He is clear that he does not believe in a greater being who will "save us from ourselves" and so he exhorts us to be kind and to "preserve and cherish the pale blue dot". How does this connect to the Golden Rule that most world religions share – the rule that exhorts us to "do unto others as you would have done unto yourself"?

Concept: Belief.

Lines of inquiry: Do we agree that, as physicist Richard Feynman said, "nothing is certain or proved beyond all doubt"?[3] Is it possible to be a scientist and believe in God without doubt? What do religion and science have in common? What separates them?

Curriculum areas: Science, philosophy, religion and ethics.

⦿ **What if ...** everything we knew about the universe and our planet was but a fraction of what is yet to be known? Which parts of science can we be certain about? Which are yet but theories? What do you think might yet be discovered? What are scientists exploring at the edge of our understanding? What kinds of minds do these scientists need to have? Could you create a text (or a film, presentation, performance, etc.) that explores all that is not yet known and understood? How would you communicate to your reader or audience what is reasonably certain and what is completely unknown in your area of inquiry?

Concept: Uncertainty.

Lines of inquiry: What is yet to be known? What has been "known" and then "unknown"?

....

2 Of particular relevance is the extract available here: http://www.planetary.org/explore/space-topics/earth/pale-blue-dot.html.
3 Feynman, R. (1956) The Relation of Science and Religion, transcript of a talk given by Dr. Feynman at the Caltech YMCA Lunch Forum on 2 May 1956. Available at: http://calteches.library.caltech.edu/49/2/Religion.htm.

Curriculum areas: Theoretical science, theory of knowledge, ethics and philosophy, debate, writing to persuade, media and film.

⊙ **What if ...** your class were invited to take part in the first human-manned mission to Mars? How long would it take to get there? Is there any hope you would ever come back? What do you expect Mars to be like in terms of weather, gravity, resources and so on? What would make someone want to go and take that risk? What would you take with you in order to (a) survive and (b) record and communicate your findings? What would you write to the people left behind who may never see you again?

Concept: Human exploration.

Lines of inquiry: Would the acclaim and adventure be worth never seeing your loved ones again? What drives human beings to want to explore?

Curriculum areas: Time, space, gravity, air and atmosphere, human belonging and belief, ethics of cost versus benefit, descriptive writing, diary writing and technical writing.

⊙ **What if ...** it was announced that the government were going to spend £200 billion on a new space programme? What might their arguments and justifications in favour of it be? What if you formed a pressure group to ask them to reconsider their decision? How might the money be better used on earth? Is spending money on space exploration ever justified when human beings are starving or dying? Argue the case for both sides before putting it to a vote. You'd need to find out details about how much space exploration costs – what would £200 billion actually fund? How does that compare with the money needed for, say, education, social care and the NHS?

Concept: Priorities.

Lines of inquiry: Is it right to spend money on space exploration when there are people suffering on earth? Do human beings have more of a responsibility towards knowledge and advancement than towards each other?

Curriculum areas: Politics and economics, distribution of wealth, space programmes, funding and spending, responsibilities in space – space junk, understanding large numbers, ethics.

a stopover

This was first delivered in a special setting with a Key Stage 3 group but could easily be adapted for primary.

The class are shown a large cardboard box. In it there are a number of objects that are old or worn – normal, everyday objects, nothing too flashy or modern-looking. Pick each object out of the box and show it to the children. Take time over this as if the objects are the most precious things on the planet. Here's an example:

"What's this? A pencil. Yes, just an ordinary pencil. It looks well used. It's much shorter than a new pencil, isn't it? It's an old pencil. It had a busy life until it was packed away in this box. It could do with sharpening. It's stubby. It might be difficult to write with now.

I wonder what stories it has written. I wonder if it ever wrote a letter. I wonder who the letter was to.

It's only a pencil, but it could hold many secrets, couldn't it? Pencils are pretty important, it seems to me.

What's this? A key …"

The important thing here is pace. The simple objects are treated with reverence, with preciousness.

If the class had to create a simple box to sum up who they are, what would they include in it? They can discuss this and perhaps compile a list of objects. They may well make these lists very personal so that the contents of the box reflect them as individuals rather than as a group, which is fine too.

The children each choose an object from the list. Ask them to stand in a circle and be ready to talk about their chosen object. Help the children by using these prompt questions:

◉ What is it?

- Is it man-made?

- Do you know where it comes from?

- What is its function?

- Why is the object useful?

- What might the object have seen in its life?

- Where would it be kept?

This process invests the children into the context.

Then a message arrives. The class have been invited to contribute to a humanity pod that is to be sent into space in the hope that it might be picked up by intelligent alien life. The contents of the pod need to reflect the positive aspects of humanity – nothing negative should be included.

The pod is a 1m² cube. Use masking tape to create the outline of the pod on the classroom floor. Think about how much space there will be inside. How will we fit everything in? What might we have to leave out? Could images be better than objects?

Could we send recordings? What messages do we want to send? The children can prepare short pieces to be recorded. They need to decide on how to organise the content. Work out the key information that needs to be included and then do paired preparation.

You don't actually need to record these pieces unless you have the technology to hand. Reading them aloud to each other would also be good. If the pieces are written up, they can be placed within the outline of the pod. A list of sounds from earth could also be included – for example, birdsong, a baby crying, a choir singing, someone laughing hysterically.

Could we include works of art? Which would we chose? Copies of famous paintings, recordings of important pieces of music, great works of literature?

How do we choose what to include and what to reject? What makes one piece of art more important than another? Discuss subjectivity and objectivity – how are we applying value to these objects?

The pod is due to be completed as soon as possible. A new message is received that shifts the emphasis of the work that has been done so far:

We need to be honest with what we are loading onto the pod.

So far you have been very positive about the things which will go inside. We now need you to take a step back and consider which *negative* aspects of humanity we should include within the cargo of knowledge. If you could issue a warning to aliens about the dangers that human beings can present, what would you say?

We need to speak truth to the universe.

Please now consider what should be added to the pod.

The launch date has been brought forward to next week.

The children might suggest a multitude of negatives about humanity. As you did at the start with the objects in the cardboard box, take the time to consider each idea. You could tap into ideas about values systems, conflict and oppression. You could think about which objects would show the negative aspects of humanity. You could repeat the process of making or reading recordings, but this time with the warnings. The class could also think about *balance*. How do the positive elements of humanity balance out the negative?

This suggested stopover could go off in many directions and, like a lot of ideas in this book, everything is open to interpretation and adaptation depending on the age of your children. When we asked an 11-year-old what five things he would send into space in a humanity pod, he said:

- A copy of *The Beano*.

- An egg.

- A picture of his cat, Basil.

- A recipe for spaghetti carbonara.

- Elliot, his mate from school.

Here are a few final suggestions for directions to take:

- Plan the public launch of the pod — what jobs need doing?
- Prepare the press release telling the story of the pod and explaining what's inside and why.
- Look at what didn't go into the pod. Why were these things rejected?
- How will we know if the pod makes contact with alien life? What is our plan if this does happen?

stepping stones

You could:

- Create a playlist of music that you feel sums up life on earth that could be broadcast into deep space.
- Decide on an inventory list for a deep space survival shop. Price your stock.
- Consider the jobs that need doing prior to a manned space launch.
- Design a diet and fitness regime for astronauts to follow while they journey in a space capsule.
- Look at the tragic accounts of the Columbia space shuttle disaster in 2003. Create contrasting journalist reports about the celebratory launch of the mission and its sad ending.
- Map out a floor plan of an exploratory deep space craft. Consider the implications that zero gravity will have on your design.
- Create a marketing campaign to promote holidays to the moon.
- Research the stories behind the naming of the constellations.
- Visit the National Space Centre (UK), the National Air and Space Museum (US) or the Euro Space Center (Belgium).

the Bedrock – the power of Narrative

According to cognitive scientist Daniel Willingham, "stories are psychologically privileged" in our minds.[4] That is to say, we are irresistibly drawn towards stories and that they can help us to remember content in a way that few other things do. It has even been shown that presenting conceptual scientific information in story form makes for better retention.[5] In each and every one of the chapters in this book, you have scenarios in which you can place much of the knowledge content of your curriculum into a dilemma-led story.

Willingham breaks down the elements of story that the human brain connects with into four C's – causality, complications, conflict and character. When these four elements are in place, children are far more likely to recall information than they are when that same information is presented in expository form.

Causality is about how events link together through consequence. It is not simply a matter of "this happened then that happened" – that is simply a narrative. Rather, the two points in time, or plot lines, are connected as consequential actions – "this happened because …", " … therefore that happened". This creates powerful memories for human beings. It was E. M. Forster who defined plot as the connected causalities within a story. In a 1927 series of lectures, later published as *Aspects of the Novel*, he pointed out that plot demands intelligence and memory on the part of the reader – they must remember incidents and create connecting threads between them – whereas a story is simply a sequence of events. It is the effort of connecting, of recognising cause and consequence, that makes causality such a powerful tool for learning.

Complications take us back to the notion of engaged confusion or, as we explored in Chapter 3, cognitive disequilibrium. It is when we're in this state – in which things are suddenly not as they once seemed, in which what we thought we knew is no longer secure, in which our sense of intellectual security is being challenged – that we are primed to learn. This is why so many of the examples throughout the book contain moral pivots – points at which children are guided into difficulty,

---

4 Willingham, Ask the cognitive scientist.

5 Arya, D. J. and Maul, A. (2012) The role of the scientific discovery narrative in middle school science education: an experimental study, *Journal of Educational Psychology*, 104(4): 1022–1032.

plots twist and turn and moral dilemmas are rife. Will we sell a house to Count Dracula? Will we chop down an ancient tree? What is precious to us? These dilemmas and questions create complications in our story, prompting deep and active engagement.

Conflict may be better considered as tension. Tension engages our emotions and puts us on high alert, making us more attentive. In real life, of course, it can be a cause of stress; tension in a story, however, is exciting. It forces emotional engagement – itself an important trigger for memory.[6] It creates pivotal moments in which key decisions have to be made – often under pressure, drawing on children's abilities to connect and consider. Tension motivates us to action – we want to resolve and progress within a story – and it allows us to bring deep problem solving into the classroom.

Character allows children to relate to and connect with other human beings. When encountering other characters, we tend to compare ourselves with them, finding points of empathy or dissonance between our own experiences, emotions and values and theirs, and judging them accordingly. The process of engaging with and considering different characters brings the real and fictional worlds closer together, allowing children to "practise" scenarios. This is powerful even if you're just reading a story. But if you are in a story, the effect is even more so, because you are not just thinking about a character, you are embodying them – an additional layer of interaction that allows for a physical as well as intellectual connection to take place. If we return to the work on embodied cognition that we explored in Chapter 1, we can see how doubly powerful this could be in getting children to remember, to feel and to make decisions.

6 Curran, A. (2008) *The Little Book of Big Stuff About the Brain: The True Story of Your Amazing Brain.* Carmarthen: Independent Thinking Press.

Chapter 7
The Wasteland

The time had come to move on. Again.

Where are these people going?

Where have they been?

Where is the life here?

What will the people find here?

Why are they not at home?

Where is home?

Why are the figures in the middle and the foreground separated from the main group?

Your own questions …

....
Download the image from www.crownhouse.co.uk/featured/uncharted-territories

The wasteland

One of the most extraordinary abilities of human beings is our capacity to settle in the most hostile environments. The spread of human life across the planet was achieved by adapting our surroundings to our needs. Unlike other species, who have adapted to their environment, we have survived by utilising resources, tools and materials to adapt the environment to ourselves. So is there such a thing as a wasteland, and what do human beings need in order to survive?

primary landmarks

◉ **What if ...** you were asked to design a factory to manufacture a product called a Thneed? The product is made from the fruit of a Truffula tree and so needs to be located close to the Truffula forest. The Truffula fruit must be boiled for hours before it releases its soft fibres. How will you conduct this process? How will it be fuelled? The boiling process produces toxic fumes that must be directed out of the factory or the workers will become ill. How will this be factored into your design? You are asked to present two options to the factory owner – a cheaper one that will simply release the fumes into the air outside, and a more expensive one that will either remove the toxins from the fumes or store the poison safely. What if the factory owner insists on the cheapest design and, over time, your factory starts to poison the environment? There are protests and newspaper articles written about your bad design. The Truffula forest dies, the factory closes and the earth is poisoned, meaning no one can live there any more. What if your team of designers was then charged with the task of cleaning up and restoring this polluted land? What would you have to do? How would you restore it? How long would it take? You can research real cases of industrial contamination to get ideas. You could also go on to read *The Lorax* by Dr. Seuss to find out more about the Truffula forests!

Concept: Responsible industry.

Lines of inquiry: What responsibilities do companies have to protect the environment? Why don't they do more?

Curriculum areas: Profit and loss – percentages and accounts, poisons and pollutants, ethics, protest and political process, writing to hide information, writing to expose and protest – bias, fact and opinion.

⊙ **What if …** you were chosen to join the crew of an expedition to Antarctica to explore the possibility of resettling human populations there? Why is the Arctic region more populated than the Antarctic? What questions would you want answered before you left? What would you take with you? What would life be like there? What materials would best withstand freezing temperatures? What questions might you be asked at a prelaunch press conference? If resettlement is a viable possibility, who would you be thinking of sending there?

Concept: Survival.

Lines of inquiry: Who owns Antarctica? Could anyone go and live there? Should there be places on earth without borders? Is Antarctica changing? What might it be like in the future?

Curriculum areas: Adaptation to environment, how to survive in very cold climates, understanding the ways in which life might be different in extreme places, ethics of colonisation and land ownership.

⊙ **What if …** a corner of the classroom turned into a snowy land with polar bears, seals and whales? What if, over a period of time, the snow started to melt so that large parts of the floor became pools or rivers? What if the polar bears came to ask you for help? How can the animals live in this place now? What are they to do? Where can they go? How would you help the polar bears to adapt to the land without snow and ice?

Concept: Survival needs.

Lines of inquiry: Why do liquids freeze? Why does ice melt? What do polar bears need to survive? How can human beings protect animals and help them to survive?

Curriculum areas: Understanding the world, social and emotional development through empathy and problem solving.

secondary landmarks

⊙ **What if ...** you were responsible for establishing a series of deep-sea research colonies in the most inhospitable and uncharted parts of the oceans? The structures need to be able to house research scientists and oceanographers from all over the world. Design these structures, thinking carefully about water pressure, temperature, light, what materials to use and the impact on the natural environment. How would the structures be maintained and how could you ensure the safety of the occupants? How does researching these dark and deep areas of our planet actually help humanity?

Concept: Resourcefulness.

Lines of inquiry: How do human beings use scientific knowledge to innovate and explore? What right do we have to occupy areas of the earth that are other species' more natural habitats? How do we ensure our desire to discover does not destroy that which we seek to understand?

Curriculum areas: Water pressure, light, density, marine life, underwater geography and geology, design, ethics.

⊙ **What if ...** you were working for a charity to place solar energy into remote villages across the African continent so that people could have power without it costing them anything? Your charity intends to supply a set of panels and a generator to as many villages as possible. How much energy could you create? What might it be used for? Your funding depends on your ability to prove that this would improve both health and educational outcomes and put people off going to live in the overcrowded cities. How would you achieve these aims and how would you prove the impact of your project? Can energy provide answers to the problems of living in inhospitable environments?

Concept: Energy.

Lines of inquiry: What is energy and how do we use it? How could we use it differently? Should energy be free?

Curriculum areas: Energy and renewables, poverty, transportation, regulations and rules, international aid and the role of governmental and non-governmental organisations.

❂ **What if …** you were asked to design an underground city for people living in highly polluted cities so that they needn't ever go outside? Look at Montreal's "underground city" model of subterranean networks – which links offices, shops, business centres and residential areas using a series of underground walkways – for inspiration. What would you need to consider? How would staying inside impact on people's physical and mental health and what measures could you take to minimise that impact? Is this solution better than tackling the pollution above ground? How will you pitch your ideas to secure the contract to build this city? What makes your design better and unique?

Concept: Population and housing.

Lines of inquiry: When we've used as much of the space above us as we can, is it possible or desirable to go below ground? What impact would living underground have on human beings? What is the relationship between natural light and human health?

Curriculum areas: Light, health, engineering, housing, population growth, innovation.

a stopover

This was initially an interdisciplinary Key Stage 3 project between the English, science and geography departments. But it could easily be adapted for any of these individual subjects in a secondary setting and for primary project work too.

Share the illustration provided at the start of this chapter with the class. Ask the children to describe what they see using single adjectives and collate them on the board. They may contribute words such as "dead", "desolate", "barren", and so on. Ask them what they notice about life in this place – is anyone or anything living there? What do they imagine the weather to be like and why? Could anything survive there? Begin to draw the children into the scene:

"Let's say we have to survive in this place. Let's say we have just arrived here. We each have a small rucksack. We've placed them to one side for now, while we look around. This is the land we have been allocated by the authorities as our new home. There is nothing here. We have only what we have brought with us in our rucksacks. It is late afternoon. What is the first thing you think we should do?"

Gather the children's thoughts – they will probably suggest building a shelter, finding food and water and having a closer look at what is there. Go back to their conversations about the weather and, taking their ideas, ask them what kind of shelter might be best, what materials we might use and how we might erect it. You may need to guide them a little here. If they initially said "it rains a lot", go back to the image: "… wouldn't there be more plants if there was lots of rain?"

Now it is time to explore what resources the group has. Ask the children to each take a sheet of A3 paper and draw and label all the things they have packed in their rucksack. The rucksack can be no bigger than their own back and whatever is in it must fit. This isn't a "magic" bag!

Model this by sharing the contents of your own rucksack – a wind-up torch, a tarpaulin, tent pegs, plastic sheets, dried fruit, an umbrella, matches, a 1 litre bottle of water, a compass and a book – Bear Grylls' *Survival Camp*. If possible, collect these objects and bring them in in a real bag – alternatively you could use images to illustrate. How might these objects be useful?

Take the children's drawings and say, "Well good, we have …" List the items and discuss how useful each of them might be. Tell them that you are going to take all of the items, as they now belong to the group, and that you'll distribute them fairly. They can keep personal belongings such as photographs and keepsakes, but not computers, phones, food or water. These must be shared among the group. Tell the children that you're going to share the contents of your own rucksack too.

Discuss the decision. Is this fair?

Taking the items they have listed, think about how to allocate them. If children have listed four tents between them, but there are 30 in the class, who gets to sleep in a tent? How big is each tent? How many people can sleep in them? How should the class decide? What other shelters could you make with what you have?

Tell the children that the priority is to build shelter for the night – we can think about everything else in the morning. Get them to design the shelters, thinking about the direction they will point in, the shape they will be, how they will stand up and stay up and anything else they think is important. You could use a compass to check direction. You could assess their understanding of direction by offering guidance such as, "The wind seems to be coming from the east and it feels quite bitter. It will be even colder tonight – make sure the openings of your shelters are not pointing east."

You may or may not decide to actually build the shelters, depending on your learning goals. You may decide to simply map out the boundary of some of the shelters with masking tape and let the children describe what they have designed. The objective is to get them thinking about the factors affecting the practicalities of the design. If heavy snow is likely, then the shelter must not have a flat top. If rain is expected, it is better not to situate it at the bottom of a hill. If it's windy, you'll want the surface to protect against the wind and not allow the cold in, but if the wind is strong such a surface might create enough resistance for the structure to be blown down. If the sun is going to be hot in the morning, some ventilation will be necessary – all this advice will largely be dictated by what the children describe and how they invent the circumstances they are in. You can build some of these variables in as the story progresses.

As the group enter their first night in this place, how are they feeling? If this were real life, what would they be thinking and fearing as they settle in this new, not very hospitable place? They could write diary entries to describe this, or you could ask them to settle as if they are trying to sleep and gently **thought track** their ideas as they lie there.

When morning comes (or the start of the next session), the children are told it is time to make an inventory of the food and water they have and to think how they are going to make it last. These amounts will depend on what they each packed in their rucksacks. Having had a chance to look back at the items on their A3 sheets, count each bottle of water as a litre and list each item of food. Remember that you brought a litre of water and some dried fruit to add to the rations. In preparation for this activity, ask the children to do some research – how much water do humans need to drink in a day? What other uses for water will they have? Can they prioritise them? Based on there being 30 children in the class, how long will the water they have with them last? How much can they each have today? You can do similar calculations with the food.

Share with them the Crisis Times website's advice about finding food in the desert and ask them to use it to make some decisions about what to do next.[1] A clear message in this text is that it is important to first secure a water supply. How might they do this? Stepping out of the story, you could introduce them to some possible scientific solutions, such as exploring how condensation works or how water sources are found before they re-enter the story to find some ideas. Again, the Crisis Times website is a good source of information.[2] You could point them to a low lying area where the ground is darker and some small plants seem to be growing. Could they build something to purify the water and make it safe to drink? How would they do this? Ask them to look at their materials – do they have what they need or can they fashion what they need from what they have?

Once they have secured a way of getting water, they can turn their attention back to food and to allocating roles and responsibilities. How will they cut into cacti? How will they capture insects and snakes? How will they test plants for edibility?

They are now ready to survive. Tell the children that we are going to create a ceremony to celebrate their resilience and survival skills. What should we do? How will we commemorate their arrival and survival here so that future generations can look back and remember their struggle? Plan this event and create it. Move into narrative, having prearranged with one child to pull out the photograph and deliver the final line:

"As the people sat around in a circle, reflecting on all they had learned so far, one of them pulled a photograph out of his pocket. He unfolded it and said:"

"It's hard to believe that this place once looked like this, you know … way back in the earlier part of the 21st century."

Share an image of a beautiful, verdant forest – there are many available online – and discuss. What has changed? Where do we think we might be in time now, if the early part of the 21st century was "way back"? What has happened in the meantime? Which of these two environments would we rather be trying to survive in?

....

1 See http://crisistimes.com/desert_food.php.
2 See http://crisistimes.com/survival_water.php.

What would we say to the people of "way back"? The children could write a letter to those people explaining how hard life is in a future without the forests.

From here you could:

⊙ Get the children to generate some philosophical questions for inquiry.

⊙ Ask the children to travel back to the early 21st century to give a speech to the UN on what they know about the future.

⊙ Organise the children as employees of a government agency that allocates land to those in need. There are three types of land: fertile, which is very rare and mostly confined to the higher areas of your country; tundra, where some plants and vegetation do grow but there are also cold winters, lots of snow and ice and few trees, situated to the far north of your country; and desert, the most inhospitable but most available, covering the lowlands and southern areas of your country. The children could generate maps to illustrate this. How would decisions be made about where to send people and why? What advice would be given to those people? If the government were to design different survival packs to equip people for each area, what would be in them? Would the people in the fertile lands have a duty towards the other areas? What would your laws be? How would you manage the movement of people? Could you design a land allocation application form?

STEPPING STONES

You could:

⊙ Create scaled drawings of shelters and settlements and research what types of shelter are most suitable in different environments.

⊙ Design and conduct scientific experiments to explore water collection, condensation and evaporation.

⊙ Write diary extracts from the points of view of people living in inhospitable environments.

⊙ Write information texts about how to survive in inhospitable environments.

⊙ Write speeches about the importance of tackling climate change.

- Research the changes our planet has gone through over time. Which areas are now desert which were once forested or populated?

- Carry out some research to develop a biological understanding of the impact of dehydration on the human body. How long can people go without water and what are the effects of dehydration?

- Research different climate zones and their native flora and fauna. How do plants and animals adapt to survive and thrive in different environments?

The bedrock – happiness and well-being

It would be fair to say that it is not just in the UK that we are witnessing an alarming rise in mental health difficulties among the young. In Hong Kong, in one month alone in 2017, five youth suicides took place and the government and media are beginning to consider the role that the education system has to play in leading children towards this catastrophic end.[3] Elsewhere across the academically high-performing regions of Asia, governments are concerned with the same problem. Health researchers Peter Anderson and Eva Jané-Llopis point out that poor mental health, and related illness, is the number one premature killer in the developed world, outlining the connection between poor mental and physical health and the associated cost to our societies.[4]

In the 2015 PISA well-being tests, the UK came 38th out of 48 countries in measures of mental health and feelings of well-being and happiness among young people – a far lower ranking than the results in English, maths and science that got so much media attention.[5] 72% of UK students felt high levels of anxiety before a

....

3   Huang, E. (2017) A spate of student suicides is forcing Hong Kong to confront its cutthroat school system, *Quartz* (13 February). Available at: https://qz.com/904483/a-spate-of-student-suicides-is-forcing-hong-kong-to-confront-its-cutthroat-school-system/.

4   Anderson, P. and Jané-Llopis, E. (2011) Mental health and global well-being, *Health Promotion International*, 26(1): 147–155. Available at: https://academic.oup.com/heapro/article/26/suppl_1/i147/686692/Mental-health-and-global-well-being.

5   Ward, H. (2017) UK pupils among the world's unhappiest, *tes* (19 April). Available at: https://www.tes.com/news/school-news/breaking-news/uk-pupils-among-worlds-unhappiest.

test even if they were well prepared, against an OECD average of 55%.[6] Perhaps one reason for this is that UK students feel motivated by the idea that they have to be "the best" to succeed, a common narrative within the education system, which puts additional pressure on them. In addition, they report being victim to higher than OECD average levels of bullying. For these and other reasons, including economic considerations, it is clear that young people's mental health and well-being is becoming a significant cause for concern for governments across the world. Yet what does our education system do to counter these difficulties, or to cause them?

Harvard University's 75-year-long Grant Study is clear in its finding that happiness is linked to strong, reciprocal human relationships, which – above any other factor – give people a sense of contentment and belonging.[7] In fact George Vaillant, one of the project's lead researchers, went so far as to summarise this enormous amount of work in five words – "Happiness is love. Full stop."[8]

What does this have to do with education and, specifically, with this book? Well, in each example we offer, children are working collegiately. They are being asked to develop strong, responsible teams who are charged with problem solving and creating. Negotiating the issues presented allows children to practise relationships, reciprocity and empathy, and to build a capacity to understand other people's points of view. Learning to listen, to consider, to understand how to meet others' needs, to be kind, to be helpful – all of these things help children to better understand how to develop the interpersonal skills that will be so important to their future well-being. But there is more than this.

Placing children in a dilemma, in which they encounter difficulty and find solutions, equips them with a sense of agency. They are not only being asked to practise resilience, which we know to be crucial to their well-being, but they are being given a chance to directly experience and design interventions that will help

6 OECD (2017) *United Kingdom: Country Note – Results from PISA 2015 (Volume III): Students' Well-Being*, p. 1. Available at: http://www.oecd.org/pisa/PISA2015-students-well-being-United-Kingdom.pdf.
7 Itkowitz, C. (2016) Harvard researchers discovered the one thing everyone needs for happier, healthier lives, *The Washington Post* (2 March). Available at: https://www.washingtonpost.com/news/inspired-life/wp/2016/03/02/harvard-researchers-discovered-the-one-thing-everyone-needs-for-happier-healthier-lives/?utm_term=.3c67606bc699.
8 Quoted in Stossel, S. (2013) What makes us happy, revisited, *The Atlantic* (May). Available at: https://www.theatlantic.com/magazine/archive/2013/05/thanks-mom/309287/.

to solve a problem. And they are being put in contexts that allow for deep thought and for joyfulness and play.

We know from studies that laughter and pleasure lower cortisol levels in the brain and relieve stress.[9] Movement, mindfulness and caring for others offer similar benefits. And these are things we need to take more seriously in our planning of teaching and learning. The price to pay otherwise is very high.

Human beings living with prolonged high levels of stress have higher levels of cortisol in their systems. It also seems that cortisol levels are higher in adolescent males than in females, impacting upon their likelihood of taking risks and placing themselves in danger.[10] Social isolation stemming from the "flight or fight" response to stress, interacting with high levels of cortisol, also leads many young adolescent men into lifelong mental illness.[11] And we know that cortisol impacts badly on episodic and verbal declarative memory systems, making it much harder for young people under stress to perform well in tests.[12]

It's clear then, that reducing stress is of vital importance to learning and to children's future success and happiness. What is the point of education if not to equip children for happy and successful lives filled with purpose, love and joy? To this end, all of the ideas presented here are centred around what educationalist Mary Myatt refers to as the "joyful spirit of collective endeavour" – a sense of coming together with common purpose to, well, just sort things out.[13]

9 Berk, L. S. et al. (1989) Neuroendocrine and stress hormone changes during mirthful laughter, *The American Journal of the Medical Sciences*, 298(6): 390–396. Available at: https://doi.org/10.1097/00000441-198912000-00006.

10 Daughters, S. et al. (2013) Gender specific effect of psychological stress and cortisol reactivity on adolescent risk taking, *Journal of Abnormal Child Psychology*, 41(5): 749–758. doi:10.1007/s10802-013-9713-4

11 Bergland, C. (2013) Cortisol: Why "the stress hormone" is public enemy no. 1, *Psychology Today* (23 January). Available at: https://www.psychologytoday.com/blog/the-athletes-way/201301/cortisol-why-the-stress-hormone-is-public-enemy-no-1.

12 Wolf, O. (2009) Stress and memory in humans: twelve years of progress? *Brain Research*, 1293: 142–154. Available at: https://doi.org/10.1016/j.brainres.2009.04.013.

13 Myatt, M. (2016) *Hopeful Schools: Building Humane Communities*. Mary Myatt Learning Limited, p. 56.

CHAPTER 8

The 300

There was no movement before him. No scent.

What does the snow leopard dream about?

The mural appears scarred. Who made these scars and why?

What does the snow leopard think about when he looks at the night sky?

Who else in the zoo looks to the stars and thinks?

What will happen to the snow leopard when he ceases being an exhibit in the zoo?

Would the snow leopard be safe if he escaped?

Your own questions …

_____

_____

_____

_____

_____

_____

Download the image from www.crownhouse.co.uk/featured/uncharted-territories

The Zoo

Animals are a source of fascination for most younger children, tapping into their curiosity about difference. Zoos offer rich contexts for learning – there is a business element, a conservation element, there are ethical considerations and, of course, there are the animals themselves. Over the years, we've both been inspired by Anthony Browne's searing book *Zoo* and in this chapter we delve deeply into human and animal behaviour as seen through his text. As with all the settings, we would encourage you to take children out to the place of inquiry – the zoo – and let them see it with new eyes.

Primary Landmarks

- **What if …** after enjoying a meal with the class, the tiger who came to tea went home and got sick? What if the next day the children are visited by an angry zookeeper? The zookeeper wants them to create a recipe book of healthy foods for animals, to prevent them from being fed the wrong thing and becoming ill. They could invite the tiger back for a healthy tea (and perhaps teach him some table manners!).

  Concept: Health and nutrition.

  Lines of inquiry: What do different species need in order to be healthy? How should we look after animals?

  Curriculum areas: Healthy eating, weighing and measuring ingredients, etiquette for guests, writing instructions and lists, writing invitations – dates and times, story maps, animal species and types of diet – carnivore, omnivore, herbivore.

- **What if …** you found out that the snow leopard longed for home? What if the painted background wall isn't a good enough substitute for his real habitat? How could you redesign the zoo to provide an appropriate climate and habitat for the animals? What if this proves to be too expensive? What would you do for the snow leopard?

Concept: Habitats.

Lines of inquiry: Is it ever right to keep something in captivity? If animals are to be kept in zoos, do we have a responsibility to replicate their natural climate as well as their habitat?

Curriculum areas: Writing accounts of the snow leopard from his point of view and his keeper's and visitors' points of view, design, scaled drawings, costings, materials, climate control technology.

◉ **What if ...** you were a team of zoo inspectors who receive a call from a worried visitor to a local zoo? The visitor reports that the animals are not being treated very well. What would you expect to see if the animals were being well cared for? After you visit the zoo, and speak with the animals, could you design an alternative and present this to the zoo trustees on the condition that they must make the changes in order to stay open? What if they can't afford it? Where will the animals go?

Concept: Protection.

Lines of inquiry: Why do zoos exist? What responsibilities do owners of animals have for their welfare? What might a zoo inspector do on a visit to a zoo? Why might someone want to own a zoo?

Curriculum areas: Animal welfare and ethics, costings (animal feed, staff salaries, and so on), calculating area, writing reports.

secondary landmarks

◉ **What if ...** you worked for an organisation commissioned by the zoo to provide all the signage, information boards and publicity material for some international visitors? You need to consider branding and communicating on paper, signs and online. You need to present the zoo in the best light and provide visitors with detailed information about the animals. You should also include more practical information such as maps, ticket prices and details about sponsoring and supporting the zoo through donations. This will all need to be in several languages.

Concept: Language and communication.

Lines of inquiry: Should we have a responsibility to make visitors feel welcome by embracing their language? What is our experience of travelling abroad – is English catered for? When we translate, do we need to give full or partial information?

Curriculum areas: Writing to inform in different languages, costings and budgeting, design (mapping walkways and routes through the zoo, locating the gift shop, cafe, etc.), branding, research into animal species and their habitats and needs.

⊙ **What if ...** you were asked to set up a breeding programme for endangered animals at a zoo? How would it work? What would you prioritise? What equipment would you need? How would it be paid for? What if technological advances meant you could bring back extinct species? Would it be ethical to do so?

Concept: Conservation.

Lines of inquiry: Do human beings have a responsibility to breed animals that are in danger of extinction? Do breeding programmes in captivity create excuses for allowing animals to become extinct in the wild? Are some animals harder to breed than others?

Curriculum areas: Reproduction, in vitro fertilisation, extinction, conservation, ethics.

⊙ **What if ...** there was an international law introduced that meant all animals in captivity had to be homed in an environment and climate that was as close to their natural habitat as possible? What would a zoo in Norway look like in comparison with a zoo in Singapore? How would the international exchange of animals take place? What kinds of procedures would have to be put in place? Which country's zoos would be the best?

Concept: Adaptation.

Lines of inquiry: How do animals adapt to climate? Does removing an animal from its natural climate impact evolution? What effects might climate change have on animals? Does a human's desire to keep an animal override the welfare of the animal?

Curriculum areas: Climate, habitat, evolution, geography and natural fauna.

a stopover

This section diverts a little from the style of previous stopovers. Rather than being a series of activities, it's really more of a close reading of a text with suggestions for stopping off points. You could layer in lots of drama activities drawn from the list in the back of the book here, or simply take these ideas to conduct a deep reading experience, perhaps leaping off into Philosophy for Children (P4C) inquiries. Unfortunately copyright prohibits us from sharing the images we refer to here, but we have described them in the order in which they appear in the book. If you are not able to get a copy, you could apply these close reading techniques and strategies to another text of your choice.

This journey takes Anthony Browne's book *Zoo* as its starting point. Never be put off using picture books – especially ones as rich as those by Browne or Shaun Tan – with Key Stage 2 and 3 children. They draw comprehension, deep thinking and problem solving out of learners of any age. This is a story about behaviour.

Give the children the first four images of the book: the headshots of the family, the journey to the zoo, the ticket office and the family entering the zoo. Ask the children to look at the images closely and talk about what they notice. Draw their attention to the animal characteristics of the people in the images. Talk about the family and how they are presented. You could create a **role on the wall** for each character. What can we infer about each character just from these images? What do we think Browne is going to ask us to think about regarding human beings and their behaviour?

Now read the text. What do the pictures give us that the words don't?

Look at how the dad's speech is described – "roared", "snarled" – what are the connotations of those words? How is the author shaping our opinion of him?

Let's imagine that as the family are entering the zoo a photograph is taken of them. What does that image look like? Get the children, in groups of four, to create it as a **still image**. If there were thought bubbles above the heads of the characters, what would they say? Ask the children to use **thought tracking** to explore further.

Ask the children to describe the atmosphere of the book and its setting so far in a single word, and justify their choice. Break into paired discussion, with each pair adding their word to the board. They could turn this into a still image if they wish.

Look at the image of the elephant. Let the children discuss the composition. Why is the barrier cutting out our view of its face? How is colour used and what does it represent? What about the door that is too small for the elephant to use? Who is the door for? What is on the floor? If the elephant could speak, would it? What would it say? The only window and source of light is above its head. Can elephants look up? Do living things need to see the sky? Turn over the page.

Look at the angle of the image of the dad. Whose point of view are we getting? How have the clouds been used to portray him as a threatening figure? Open up a conversation about power. How do adults talk to children? Is "because I said so" a reasonable response? What else might be said? How is language used to control others? You could explore the nature of rules, why we need them and whether it is best to explain the reasons behind them or not.

Now look at the image of the giraffes. Again, how has Browne used colour and shape in this image to convey the giraffes' situation? What adjectives would the class use to describe the living conditions of the animals? If the class were to redesign this enclosure, what would they change? What is Browne suggesting about the importance of the animals by making them blend into their background? Turn the page.

Let's begin to think about attitudes. What is the dad's attitude towards the tiger? How does it contrast with the mum's? Having seen this image, would the children add anything to their roles on the wall? Look at the litter – what is the family's attitude towards the environment and their responsibility for it?

In pairs, get the children to think about a conversation that might take place if a zoo warden asked dad to pick up the litter and then how the conversation would go if he asked mum – they can do this in role or in writing. How would the responses differ? What might the consequences of each reaction be? How are the boys learning from their parents?

The boys are getting hungry. Do our physical needs affect our behaviour? What is casting the large shadow? Why is it just watching?

Look at the image of the tiger. Which has most power – the butterfly or the tiger? Which one is free? Does captivity remove your strength? Why is the grass greener on the butterfly's side? (You can see how this might link to wider notions of freedom.)

Now switch to the image of the rhino. Again you can talk about the use of colour and texture. Look at the speaker in the wall. Get the children to create or describe the sounds that are coming out of the speaker. Who is the speaker for?

Who is the adult in this family? Look at the angle that the image of the dad has been drawn at. Again, he is described in animal terms – he "howls". Contrast this with the penguins. Why are these penguins not funny? Look at the one in the top right hand corner. You might contrast this with footage of how penguins behave in the wild and ask the children to compare the two, either in speech or in writing.

The boys' favourite part of the day is eating junk food in the cafe and visiting the gift shop. They then, "had to go and see the polar bear. It looked really stupid." What does this say about their values in terms of what they think is entertaining? Why do you think the boys are not interested in or sympathetic to the animals? In what other ways do we as human beings become blinded to the suffering of others? Explore the concept of bystander apathy with the children.

Look at the image of the polar bear. Do we agree with the boys? Does the polar bear look stupid? How else might we describe him? Do we think the white substance he is walking on is really ice? Is it acceptable to take an animal out of its natural habitat and climate? If we artificially recreate a habitat, is it for the visual benefit of the visitors or the welfare of the animal?

We now see the family from the animal's point of view. Who is really caged? How have they been presented to us as people looking in on them as an exhibit? Do we think that the mum is trapped? Why does one boy look more like a monkey than the other does?

How are the family represented in the image of the baboons? Who is who? Look at the mum's hair and the baboons' fur. Why is the wall stained with marks from their tails? Are the boundaries between humans and animals becoming more confused at this point in the story?

Look at the image of the crowd. What do the children notice? Prompt them – how do the boys echo their parents? Compare the image of the man in the bowler hat with René Magritte's *Son of Man*. Why might Browne have incorporated this intertextual reference here? Research Magritte's painting – who might the man represent? Going back to the image in the text, look at the image of the camera – what does the eye represent? How is our human nature being examined in this image? Get the children to describe it and to consider the sounds in that space. And contrast that with the solitary orangutan. What is the double meaning of "miserable thing"?

The dad is now fully transitioning into animal mode. Look at the mum's face. What is she thinking and feeling? How is the mum mirrored in the gorilla? What is her function in the family? She says, "I don't think the zoo really is for animals, I think it's for people." Do you agree with her? What are zoos for?

In the final images we enter dreamscapes. Are the boys trapped and destined to become their parents? If they are trapped, who made the trap? Can it be broken and can they escape? How do human beings escape from difficulty and from their past? Is it possible for the boys to rise above the dark, entrapped land in the final image and soar like the birds in the sky?

So much of this work is discussion-based and led by questions. It's up to you where you take it. This could be a springboard into a unit of work on nature versus nurture; on resilience; on captivity and freedom (both human and animal). The class might want to explore a particular aspect. Or they might simply want to explore how we could make better zoos. Whichever route you take, you've taught them to notice, to look more deeply and to link surface details with bigger themes and ideas. And, of course, these techniques and skills can be applied with any other text too.

stepping stones

You could:

- Write information leaflets for visitors to the zoo.

- Write diary entries as animals and visitors.

- Write witness statements as all kinds of objects in the zoo – the walls of cages, waste bins, benches …

- Write job descriptions and adverts for animal carers.

- Create fundraising and marketing communications.

- Create budgets and spreadsheets to plan the zoo's finances.

- Create designs for a remodelling of the zoo, including enclosures, cafes and shops.

- Design and stock the cafes and shops. What would be on the menu? What would you sell?

- In role as protesters who disagree with zoos, make leaflets to convince others to share your views.

- Research the needs of animals – their care, their diet, their exercise and their mating needs. Is it possible for a zoo to meet all of their needs?

- Visit a zoo.

The Bedrock – The Importance of Picture Books and Visual Literacy

It is 2013. The room is silent. A class of 11-year-olds are poring over a book, annotating feverishly as they go:

"Wishing time could stop and life could stay like this forever."

"The chip in the teapot suggests that the family are poor and struggling to make ends meet."

"Even the way they hang up their belongings shows how close they are – how terrible it would be if they were separated."

The children are looking at the opening images of Shaun Tan's *The Arrival* and they are captivated. Over the course of the half term, they explore the issue of immigration, covering the concepts of plurality, tolerance and migration (and distinguishing between refugees, asylum seekers and economic migrants). They write essays, stories, diary entries, informative texts, job applications, tourist guides, imaginary laws; all stimulated by this most rich of books – a book with no words at all. "I think this might be the hardest book I've ever read," quips one.

We underestimate the power and importance of picture books in our haste to create readers. But readers are more than decoders. They are archaeologists, painstakingly digging for meaning, intention and purpose. A great picture book allows these skills to develop at a very early age.

Colin McNaughton's *Suddenly!*, for example, teaches young children the beautiful comic potential of juxtaposition. The anticlimactic words, positioned next to the dramatic images of the foolhardy wolf, have delighted children for years. But they also teach the value of looking closely and the idea that things are not always what they seem. All great picture books do this.

In this chapter, we drew upon Anthony Browne's *Zoo* – a picture book masterpiece, a text that skilfully introduces children to the important literary notions of dramatic irony and subtext by allowing them to flit between image and text and to make connections and disconnections between the two. Without the images, the polar bear is stupid, the father less threatening and the animals boring, rather than bored. Reading the images allows children to develop the vital skills of analysis that will be crucial to their future studies, not only of literature, but also of art and of source material in other subjects. This process will equip them with the skills to look beyond the surface of images in the news – to seek truth, verification, interest and deeper meaning. Picture books are not in any way superficial and they should not be limited to the early years and Key Stage 1 – in our opinion, we should continue to use high-quality picture books throughout secondary school and particularly as a segue into media studies and art.

Why? Well, because we are beginning to better understand the importance of images in supporting memory. When new information can be spread across a number of areas – including what psychologists Alan Baddeley and Graham Hitch call the visuo-spatial sketchpad – memory is greatly enhanced and cognitive overload in working memory reduced.[1] So having images working simultaneously with text makes for better retention, thus aiding comprehension. In addition to this, the visual centres in the brain are a key element in creativity. According to neuroscientist Anna Abraham, during a creative process the brain will retrieve information from across a range of areas – visual, linguistic, spatial and limbic (emotional) – and find ways of connecting stimuli from those areas in new ways.[2] Ensuring that children are offered a rich sensory diet in school allows them to draw from across these experiences when faced with a problem or with the need to invent or innovate. The creative mind will switch between the generative and the analytical, the emotional and the rational, the visual, spatial and linguistic, in order to push new thinking, ideas and products forward. Offering children the opportunity to interact with rich texts which activate as many parts of the brain as possible can only be seen as a good thing: this is brain food.

Pushing children too quickly from picture to word-based texts undermines their capacity to learn that images can be as complex and multilayered as language can. It cuts them off from a rich source of information and beauty. We'd argue that beautiful illustration, working in conjunction with well-crafted text, creates the richest kind of book of all. A child who has been steeped in these multidimensional

....

1   Baddeley, A. D. and Hitch, G. (1974) Working memory. In G. H. Bower (Ed.), *The Psychology of Learning and Motivation: Advances in Research and Theory*, Vol. 8. New York: Academic Press, pp. 47–89.
2   Abraham, *The imaginative mind*.

books will, when they encounter written texts, draw on the visual centres in their brains to imagine the words into being. This process is part of dual coding.[3] In addition, readers tend to develop an emotional link to the written word by seeing and feeling the images words generate in their minds – the "inward eye" of Wordsworth's "bliss of solitude". Let's not then, in our rush to create the kinds of readers who can pass tests, undermine the development of a lifelong love of reading by devaluing the very texts that build those skills a great reader has. Let's champion the picture book.

---

3   For an example of this model, see http://www.instructionaldesign.org/theories/dual-coding.html.

chapter 9
The cave

The cave would now be their home. Would the secrets of the stone-flushed water offer them eternal youth?

Deep in the cave, the figure sees something glowing across the water. What is it they see? Who has left it there to be found?

From where has the water travelled?

What (if anything) grows in the darkness?

What is reflected in the water?

What are the shapes on the roof of the cave? How long have they been there?

Your own questions ...

_____

_____

_____

_____

_____

_____

_____

_____

Download the image from www.crownhouse.co.uk/featured/uncharted-territories

The cave

From cavemen to cavers, offering shelter and adventure, caves are full of mystery and life. Our human history is rooted in them – look, for example, at the prehistoric cave art that can be found throughout the world. To this day, people still live in homes which extend out of caves. The vastness of time is writ large in the formations of stalactites and stalagmites. A visit through cave systems, for example the ones found at Castleton in Derbyshire, reveals how natural caves can be extended and developed by humans for mining, punctuated by tragic tales of children dying of tallow candle poisoning as they tried to light their way in the darkness. Who can fail to be fascinated by 40,000-year-old cave drawings, depicting life in an ancient time? In this chapter, we whet your appetite for venturing into the darkness.

primary landmarks

⊙ **What if ...** you were a group of anthropologists with a time machine who decided to go back to the Stone Age to observe an ancient tribe and learn more about their lives? Before you travel through time, what rules would you establish? Should you interfere or interact with the past? Should you remain hidden? Should you take anything away with you? What would a contract for a time traveller look like? What might it say? When you are ready to go, what date would you set on your time machine and what location? You observe a prehistoric family in their daily life. As an anthropologist, what notes would you write? How would you describe their interactions, their tools, their meals? How are they making fire? Who is hunting, who is gathering? What do their children do? If you visit a cave one evening you might find that the entrance has been blocked. Inside, a group of women are burning something on the fire – the smoke makes them hallucinate. They start to paint ... but what are they painting? Look closely and describe the images. Why are these paintings made? Why are they made by women? What do they represent? What is the smoky substance? You might have other excursions – for example, you might witness a hunt. Describe the animals and the landscape. When you return to the present to share your findings, how will you do this? Prepare a presentation for an audience who have been invited to hear about your first time travel adventure.

Concept: Understanding our history.

Lines of inquiry: If we could visit the past, what would our ethical responsibilities be? How has humankind used materials resourcefully in its development? Why paint on walls of caves? Is art a necessity to humans?

Curriculum areas: Timelines, scale of time – human time versus geological time, the role of art in early life, understanding how humans survived in the past, writing accounts and reports.

⊙ **What if ...** when walking on the beach one day, a child hears rumbling and looks up to see some rocks falling from the cliff side? He sees the rocks fall, blocking off a small cave. When the adults return, they say it is safe, that the cave was empty, but the boy thinks he saw the face of a man at the entrance to the cave. He thinks the man may be trapped inside. He returns the next day, but there is a sign at the bottom of the cliff which says, "Danger. Do Not Enter." The boy calls out towards the cliff face, "Hello! Is anybody there?" He hears a faint sound ... "Help!" What should the boy do? Should he go to help himself or should he try to persuade someone else to help him? Who should he turn to for help? If you worked for a rescue organisation, what equipment might you need to help someone in such a landfall? What precautions would you take? Would you risk your life to help another? Would you believe the boy? You could plan the rescue from the point of view of the organisation or from the point of view of the boy. Finally, who is the mysterious man in the cave?

Concept: Rescue.

Lines of inquiry: What are the dangers of caves and cliff faces? How might someone who is trapped be rescued?

Curriculum areas: Coastal erosion, rescue services, problem solving, creative writing and writing newspaper articles.

⊙ **What if ...** when threatened with extinction by knights in shining armour, all the dragons in the world cast a mighty spell which used up the last of their magic? The spell was a shrinking spell that reduced them all to the size of the tiniest insect. They fled into thousands of crevasses in caves around the world and there they have remained to this day. Until now. What if you were to receive an ancient letter with an instruction on it? The instruction tells you how to restore the dragons to their original size and informs you that the person who did this would be the Dragon King – the dragons forever in their debt. Could you write the letter? Would you release and resize the dragons? What might be the benefits? What might be the dangers? What would you do?

Concept: Power.

Lines of inquiry: Would you take power, even if it might mean putting others in danger? Do humans have a greater right to life than other species?

Curriculum areas: Creative writing – accounts of the dragons and knights, letter writing, designing rules and regulations to enable humans and dragons to coexist.

secondary Landmarks

⊙ **What if ...** you were a mountain rescue team that specialised in rescuing cavers? Despite recent weather warnings and landslides, a local network of caves has been entered by a group calling themselves the Spelunkers. One of the Spelunkers is the son of a high-profile politician. As predicted, the storm has led to flooding in the caves, destabilising the walls and trapping the cavers inside. You have been called in to rescue them. You will have to develop detailed drawings of the cave network and decide how to get to the trapped cavers. You will have to plan your equipment and strategy and consider possible problems. You might have to give information to the press. And afterwards, you might have to report on what happened. How might the Spelunkers be portrayed in the media? As irresponsible timewasters or adventurous heroes? How might this portrayal be affected by the status of the group member's politician father?

Concept: Civic responsibility.

Lines of inquiry: Should people who have put their own lives in danger and taken unreasonable risks be made to pay for their rescue? Do we, as a society, encourage others to take risks for the entertainment value? How are cave networks formed and what dangers do they present?

Curriculum areas: Geology, geography, newspaper report writing, crisis planning, ethics, costings.

◉ **What if …** in a cave, deep in the Scottish mountains, sits a man? He is watching a spider spin her web. The man looks tired and beaten. His kilt is dirty, his leather water container empty. He has no food. His face and legs are bruised and covered with dried blood. He is alone. But he watches the spider intently. She spins a thread and tries to swing across the rocks on it, but it breaks. Again, she tries, and again. Eventually she succeeds and the web begins to be spun. The man's expression changes. His jaw sets. He straightens up. "If at first you don't succeed …" he mutters. What if this – the opening scene of your story – begins your retelling of the tale of Robert the Bruce? What if this narrative was the start of a series of stories about people who have faced failure and overcome it?

Concept: Resilience.

Lines of inquiry: If at first you don't succeed, is it wise to try again? Is there benefit in failure? Is it true that the only real failure is giving up?

Curriculum areas: Resilience and growth mindset – sharing stories of difficulty and adversity, scriptwriting and performance, historical figures, legends and how they compare with historical fact.

◉ **What if …** there was a great drought? What kinds of activities that you take for granted now would become difficult? Could you rank, in order of importance, all the uses for water that would gradually have to be eliminated until you were left with just one – to drink? What if the drought was so bad that even finding water to drink was difficult? What if you worked for an organisation given the task of finding water? There is a possibility that there may be an underground source – an aquifer – within a network of caves. But the caves are unstable, they are like a labyrinth and many people have been lost in them. How would you go about exploring the caves and finding out if indeed there was water below ground? How would you get the water out? And who would you give it to?

Concept: Distribution of resources.

Lines of inquiry: What is an aquifer? How does it get its water supply? What do human beings need fresh water for? How can we save water and reduce our dependency on fresh water sources? How are other countries using other sources of water to do this? Who controls water supply? Is it right that we should pay for a resource that we need in order to live? If we could control the air supply, do you think we would have to start paying for it? What right do we have to "own" nature?

Curriculum areas: Science of desalination, geography, ethics, business.

a stopover

This would be suitable as an interdisciplinary activity for either primary or Key Stage 3.

The class enter to find that there is a chair in the centre of the classroom on which rests an old canvas bag. How can we find out who the owner of the bag is? One child is asked to look inside the bag. As they move to it, the class is invited to speculate on who the owner of the bag is. A man? A woman? A child? The bag looks weathered and well-travelled. Where in the world might it have been? Could this be an adventurer's bag? Agree that it is. Use **role on the wall** to begin to build a picture of the adventurer. What do you think they might look like? How old might they be?

Open the bag and reveal the contents: a paintbrush, a notebook, a pencil, some small tools and, most importantly, a piece of folded paper representing a map. What additional information do these objects give us in terms of building a picture of the adventurer?

You receive a text message:

Glad you can make it – see you soon. Have you got my bag? Are you bringing those people you said could help with you?

You reveal to the class that you know the adventurer and that he needs your help. You have responded to his invitation to meet him at the mouth of a hidden cave on the outskirts of town. You could pause to invite the children to ask you questions about the adventurer, Doctor Cross. Allow a few moments' thinking time for the children to develop meaningful questions.

Another text arrives:

They'll need to come into the cave with me. Make sure they have everything they need to be safe and useful.

How can we stay safe in the cave?

What might Doctor Cross mean by "useful"?

Are we helping him do something that is illegal?

Who could we check with?

Add to the role on the wall – what more have we learned about Doctor Cross?

Move the chair aside and throw the bag over your shoulder saying, "I'll talk as Doctor Cross." Gather the children around: they can listen to what the adventurer wants them to do via **teacher in role**.

"You can't see it because it's so overgrown, but underneath all this vegetation is a small opening in the rocks which leads to a network of caves. I last stepped into the caves 50 years ago, but I didn't get very far. The caves are not famous but according to all accounts – and there aren't many – there are spectacular huge open caverns and uncharted tunnels. I have an unfinished map courtesy of an explorer who began to chart it over 100 years ago. He never finished the job and I certainly can't do it alone. Will you help me find out the secrets of these most ancient caves?"

The class can draw the ancient, unfinished map of the network of caves. What might such an old map look like? Would it be drawn from above, as a bird's eye view, or from the side, to show the depth of the caverns and tunnels? Or both? How would it use scale to show distance? What kinds of symbols would it use? How might it be labelled? What are the names of some of the caverns? Are there stalactites and stalagmites? Underground lakes? What did the old explorer name them?

You are now at the point where you are nearly ready to enter the cave. Are there any safety precautions you should take so that, if there is an emergency or you are separated from the group, you can find your way back to the entrance? What's inside your rucksack? Get the children to list these items on sticky notes and pack them, while explaining to you or a peer the purpose of each one.

Gather the children together and explain that you are about to lift the curtain of vegetation and go into the cave. Warn them that the first 20 metres or so is cramped – the roof is low and the rocks are sharp. There may be bats living inside – startling them would be unwise. Be as quiet as you can. The floor is uneven. There may be a carpet of bat droppings. It may smell. The opening of the cave is narrow. They need to keep their heads down, their elbows in and keep moving. Once they are safely through and in the first cavern there will be more room. You could use music or sound effects to create atmosphere. You could darken the room. Ask the children to hunch together and freeze as if they are in the narrow passageway on the way into the cave network. Ask them to **thought track**. Are they nervous, claustrophobic, excited? What do they think they might discover next?

Unfreeze them and tell them that they are now safely through the passageway and that the difference could not be more stark. It is as if they are in a fairy palace or a cathedral – an enormous underground chamber with a still lake reflecting the spectacular stalactites. Give the children a moment with their notebooks to describe what they can "see".

Explain, using teacher in role as the explorer, that the group needs to get to a smaller cave across the lake. But how will they cross the water? Ask the children to think of different ways. They can design structures or test to see how deep the water is. These ideas can be shared and discussed before the next stage of the journey is settled on.

On crossing the water successfully they find an old lantern placed on top of a note.

The note reads:

Turn back.
There are hands in the darkness.

We recognise the writing as that of the explorer from years before: it is the same handwriting as is on our ancient map.

What is the explorer warning against?

Do we want to turn back?

Why might the old explorer have wanted to put off future travellers?

Let the children decide, but clearly the intention is for them to keep going! If in doubt, sink their boat or block their exit to keep them moving forward.

When we do step forward, we find an image on the ancient wall.

Ask the children what they think they are looking at. Is it a painting? Who is the painter? Who do the hands belong to? What should we do now? How important a discovery is this? Do we have a duty to share this finding, or should we, like the old explorer did, seek to keep it a secret? Why would we do this?

If the children decide to share the news, they could write newspaper reports about their discovery and even set themselves up as a trust to manage visitors to the site. If they choose to keep it a secret, they could write diary entries about their discovery, how they feel and why they don't want other people to see it. Either way, they could research the ways in which cave dwellers created images historically and why they did this.

As with all the stopover scenarios, there are many directions in which you could take this next, depending on the children's interests. You could:

⊙ Talk about sites in the world that have been protected, and ones that have been plundered or ruined.

⊙ Discuss the pros and cons of publicising the cave and its art.

⊙ Deliver the children a letter from an archaeological society claiming ownership over the site and forbidding them from entering the cave again. Discuss their reaction. Is this fair? Will they obey?

⊙ Consider who the old explorer was. Create a history and a timeline for him, including other discoveries he made. Does he have any living descendants?

⊙ Write a list of protocols to be adhered to when navigating this particular cave.

⊙ Gather at the mouth of the cave and look out. What can be seen today? A road? Lights and houses in the distance? Electricity pylons and communication satellites? What if you stood at the mouth of the cave in prehistoric times, what would you see then?

⊙ Supposing experts have dated the paintings as being roughly 40,000 years old, research what life would have been like then for the people who left these marks.

STEPPING STONES

You could:

⊙ Explore whether it is a good idea to have a fire in a cave. How would you avoid suffocating?

- Examine how the whole carcass of an animal might have been used in ancient times and what each part would be used for. Can we see any evidence of this in cave drawings and art?

- Explore how ancient people told the time of day or the time of year. What kinds of rituals and beliefs did they have? What can cave drawings tell us about this?

- Find out about how ancient structures were designed with time in mind (e.g. Stonehenge, the Great Pyramids, etc.). How did mankind move away from cave dwelling to become builders?

- Create timelines, diary entries and cave drawings of your own to depict life in the past.

- Find out how caves are formed and how long it takes for stalactites and stalagmites to form.

- Create a dream holiday brochure for cavers.

- Visit a cave.

The bedrock – the uncomfortable matter of complexity

"You dig deeper and it gets more and more complicated and you get confused and it's tricky, it's hard ... but it's beautiful."

Brian Cox[1]

In the same way that quantum physicists have discovered that the more we probe, the more unpredictable and surprising the subatomic particle world is, neuroscientists have begun to acknowledge and celebrate the incredible complexity of the human brain. Established theories, such as the functions of the left and right

1 See http://www.bbc.co.uk/sn/tvradio/programmes/horizon/broadband/tx/gravity/highlights/index_textonly.shtml.

hemispheres of the brain, are debunked as soon as technology can catch up to disprove them. And no one minds, for science – proper, pioneering, experimental, happy-with-uncertainty science – is as excited by being proven wrong as it is by being proven right. Professor Brian Cox goes as far as to say that, "Certainty is not something to be valued – it is the road back to the caves. We may have taken this for granted over the last several decades, and one of the reasons you're seeing the rise of certainty, perfectly illustrated by Donald Trump, is that people are not really being taught how to think."[2] Yet in education at the moment, we seem to be obsessed with the desire for certainty, exemplified by the growth of research lead positions in schools and the prevalence of the EEF's toolkit – a useful resource for teachers, no doubt, but one that is in danger of being used to avoid engaging with any idea that is not yet "proven" to work.

Our minds are complex adaptive systems. And what that means, as neuroscientist Susan Greenfield explains, is that our brains, like all complex adaptive systems, are more than the sum of their parts.[3] Even when we separate out individual components – working memory, visual and spatial centres and so on – we cannot predict how the whole will work together with a great degree of certainty. And classrooms too are complex adaptive systems – all those complex human beings coming together in an environment that offers multiple possibilities and distractions: from wind to wasps to windows. All this action and interaction means that, in spite of our best efforts, we can never fully predict what the outcomes of our lessons will be, other than that the lessons will (hopefully) end.

Of course, there are those who argue that you can limit the variables enough to create conditions which are closer to certainty, but to do so is to run the risk of limiting experience and possibility. This is one of the reasons why Professor Gert Biesta describes the very process of proper education as a "beautiful risk".[4]

To offer a real education, deeply and wholly, we must be able to find possibility in complexity, rather than threat. We must be brave and embrace the unexpected, the uncertain and the possible. Children thrive in this mess. They are closer than we are to uncertainty because they are constantly discovering things for the first time.

....

2   Quoted in MacKenzie, S. (2016) Professor Brian Cox: education is as important to security as missile defence, *The Big Issue* (28 November). Available at: https://www.bigissue.com/interviews/professor-brian-cox-education-important-security-missile-defence/.

3   Greenfield, S. (2011) *You and Me: The Neuroscience of Identity*. London: Notting Hill Editions.

4   Biesta, G. (2013) *The Beautiful Risk of Education*. Boulder, CO: Paradigm.

They will embrace uncertainty and newness if they are physically and emotionally safe.

Of course, there has to be guidance. But imagine your lesson as a city break: you are in Paris and you want to go to the Louvre. You could set off without a map, get lost and discover lots of new things on your journey, but you may never get to where you wanted to go. Some of your party might figure it out and get there, but most will not. They will not "discover" the Louvre.

On the other hand, you could take the metro. You'd get from A to B as expediently as possible, but you wouldn't really know how the Louvre fits into the wider geography of the city, and you'd miss out on the opportunity to see wonderful things along the way.

Or you have a map. You can walk and meander off course when things take your interest but, ultimately, you will end up where you want to be. You'll learn what you set out to at your destination, but you'll have learned more on the way too – some of it planned and predictable, and some of it unexpected.

This third way seems to us to be the most sensible method of navigating through uncertainty while not losing the joy of possibility. Perhaps this is a route between the binaries of traditional and progressive, fact and imagination and rigour and freedom?

Chapter 10

The Theme Park

The stars looked down on derelict memories.

Who sat in the seats of the ride?

Who might the girl be, high up on the ride?

Who owns the key that starts the ride?

Is the ride asleep?

Why did the designer draw eyes in the paintwork of the ride?

Your own questions ...

_____

_____

_____

_____

_____

_____

_____

_____

_____

_____

Download the image from www.crownhouse.co.uk/featured/uncharted-territories

The Theme Park

Theme parks are places where play and fear combine. Where danger hides behind safety notices, where horror stories like to lurk. Theme parks are dreams come true and nightmares made real. But they are also places where science marries art to conceive a child called commerce. Places where forces and physics link with imaginative design, conceptual art and creativity. They are ideal places to move from STEM to STEAM (science, technology, engineering, arts and maths) in the curriculum and to link these areas of learning to the real world of children's experiences, showing them the work, thought and knowledge that lies beneath a good day out.

Primary Landmarks

⊙ **What if ...** you contrasted a visit to a modern theme park with a 19th century fairground? Imagine stepping back in time to visit a Victorian fairground. What would you see and hear? Are there stalls selling different foods? What attractions and rides are there? How is the information offered about them different? What do the signs say? The Victorian fairground would feature the technology of its time. What technology is used in theme parks today? Create a modern theme park experience that celebrates the Victorian fairground. What would you not be able to include and why? What has replaced the "freak show" and why?

Concept: Changing values.

Lines of inquiry: Is humankind getting more kind? What kinds of things did the Victorians think were acceptable that we would no longer tolerate in terms of the way we treat people who are different to us or animals?

Curriculum areas: Ethics and values, the Victorian period, writing to inform and to protest, mechanics, light and sound.

◉ **What if ...** you were asked to create a new theme park in a run-down part of an industrial town? It is hoped that the theme park will create new jobs in the area. What kinds of jobs would it create? What would the theme of your park be? Could it link to local history, people or stories? How would it be different and draw people in? Map out your theme park and design some rides. In groups, think about the safety regulations of your rides. What kinds of forces affect your rides? How are they powered? How do people feel on them? Write descriptions of your rides for the park brochure. How can you use plants and design elements to make your theme park a more attractive place?

Concept: Entertainment.

Lines of inquiry: How has work changed over time? What kinds of skills and knowledge are required for different jobs? How can we use science for entertainment?

Curriculum areas: Forces and motion, design and technology, economic regeneration, local history and geography, employment and qualifications, applying for jobs, understanding pay, how work changes with technology.

◉ **What if ...** all the rides in your theme park were named after and shaped like animals? What rides would you design? Create a map of the theme park and mark all the rides on it. What if they came to life at night?

Concept: Imagination.

Lines of inquiry: Which animals are fast and which are slow? Which can fly? How would you make theme park rides look like animals? How would you give the rides the qualities and characteristics of the different animals? What would living theme park rides do when no one was looking?

Curriculum areas: Storytelling, understanding the natural world and how different animals move, understanding speed, mapping and scale.

secondary landmarks

⊙ **What if ...** you were asked to design a ride that brings together contrasting concepts from the world of physics? It needs to teach people about physics by creating real physical experiences. What would it look like? What would it feel like? Which key scientific concepts would your ride explore? What materials would you require? How explicit would the scientific concepts be? Create a pitch to explain your idea, using visuals.

Concept: Understanding the world.

Lines of inquiry: How can we use entertainment to bring better scientific understanding to people? Is this more effective than formal education? How do you explain complex material in an accessible way?

Curriculum areas: Physics, communicating concepts and ideas through explanation, impact of forces on the human body, safety and regulations.

⊙ **What if ...** following a much-publicised tragedy on a theme park ride, you are charged with the rebranding and relaunching of it to a sceptical public? You have fixed the problem with the original ride and tested it repeatedly but people still avoid it. Do you choose to close, rebrand, rename or rebuild it and why?

Concept: Perception.

Lines of inquiry: How do we reassure people and make them feel safe? How is language used to reassure and to persuade? To what extent is honesty the best policy in business? Does one bad incident impact on people's perceptions of the whole or are our memories short?

Curriculum areas: Writing to persuade, language as power, newspaper report writing – bias and inference, branding, logos, corporate identity, covert and overt prestige – could the macabre be a selling point to certain subcultures?

⊙ **What if ...** you were a local council planning department and a developer petitioned to build a new theme park on a piece of farmland? The existing access roads are rural and narrow but the site is only three miles from a major motorway and also near a ferry port. It is two miles from a town that has struggled with high levels of unemployment. What would be the case for and against the theme park? Who might give testimony at a public meeting? If the plans were to go ahead, what would the impact on the local area be? What signage and infrastructure would be needed? How would recruitment be carried out? What consideration would have to be given to the needs of local wildlife? Is it possible to have an eco-friendly theme park? How would visitors arriving at the ferry port or travelling past on the motorway be encouraged to visit?

Concept: Infrastructure.

Lines of inquiry: Do human needs (like employment) take precedence over environmental considerations? Are future consequences always fully explored in planning decisions? Are there "ideal" sites for new developments?

Curriculum areas: Social geography, business, environment, lateral thinking, problem solving, writing to persuade, signage, speaking to persuade, protest, mapping out space, planning regulations, road planning, public transport planning, balancing needs – employment versus protecting the countryside.

a stopover

This session was originally taught to primary children in a special behavioural setting. It can easily be adapted for mainstream primary settings or for Key Stage 3, particularly focusing on the issue of transport links to the theme park and the impact on the local environment.

The children enter the room to find a large masking tape grid on the floor. Tell them that they are looking at an area of beautiful countryside. It represents the land on which you propose to build a new theme park, but the class don't need to know that yet. Using photographs of fields and plants, rivers, dirt tracks, farm houses and other scenes of rural life, invite the class to arrange the images inside the outline to build up a picture of this piece of the countryside. Ask them to explain why they have chosen to place their images where they have. Talk about the images of nature and the images of people's impact on the land – the buildings and the farm machinery. Ask the children what they think the landscape was like before people settled there.

Ask the children to write examples of something that might spoil this place on sticky notes. If they need prompting you could say this might be either an object or a building. Depending on how they are doing, you might need to model ideas, and you could do this using sticky notes or images. You could suggest, for example, a rusty, broken-down car, or litter, or a fast-food outlet. You can find lots of images of seemingly inappropriate additions to beautiful sites online if you need inspiration – for example, the Great Pyramids viewed through the window of a Pizza Hut!

Once they've written down their "spoilers", let the children place the sticky notes on the grid. Discuss how these things might have got there, why they spoil the landscape and how they might be removed. Then take away the sticky note spoilers and admire the beautiful site together.

At this point, introduce a new point of tension. Take a look at the map created inside your masking tape grid and say to the class:

"… and this, colleagues, is the proposed site for the development of a new theme park. It doesn't have a name yet but this is where it will be located."

If there is dissent in the class in that they are unhappy with the development of the land, ask them to come up with reasons why. Pause while they justify why they think what they think. There is a choice here for you and, indeed, for the children. You could ask them if they would like to go along the route of objection and establish themselves as a local environmental protest group or if they'd like to go into role as theme park designers. Either way, they'll end up exploring the case for both sides eventually. In our experience though, most children can't resist the temptation of designing a theme park, even if they feel conflicted about the destruction of the landscape. For that reason, we'll explore the latter option in more depth here.

The class are asked: "If we are going to create a theme park that isn't an ugly menace on the landscape, what do we need to think about?" This can lead into some discussion about environmental impact. Suggest that this theme park is going to be as environmentally friendly as possible. What might that mean for the designers? Do we need a stronger educational slant for our theme park? Should we invite some scientists and environmentalists along to advise us? This is one way in which you can bring in their counter arguments and thoughts about protest.

In our theme park, what attractions do we hope to offer? The children's suggested attractions might blur into other themes such as fairgrounds and zoos – these ideas can be discussed and incorporated as you see fit. Ask the class to draw their proposed attractions on paper. Can they also think about what to call the rides? How can we make them sound exciting and attractive?

Remove the rural images from the masking tape grid. Begin placing the rides within the grid, with each child choosing what they think is the best location. You can make this quite ritualistic by asking each child to say "I'm placing my ride here because …" as they add their drawing. Give them time to think before they do this, so they can come up with a reason.

When all the rides are in place, ask the class what else their theme park will need – for example, a car park, toilets, disabled access routes, customer services and so on. Draw these, and place them on the grid. The car park is an interesting one as it should probably not be much smaller than the theme park itself. Why would this be? And does this conflict with their environmental aims? How might the local environmentalists feel about this? Might they mount a protest? There are also implications for the surrounding roads. What are those implications? If we are going to ensure visitors can arrive using public transport, what might we have to consider? Is our site near existing bus routes or rail networks or would we need to look more closely at the surrounding infrastructure? Our theme park will also need a name and an advertising campaign – perhaps we could even record an advert for television. We will need to write a list of ticket prices, including any special reductions we will offer.

Ask the class to imagine that you have now successfully designed and built the theme park and it is up and running. What jobs need doing to ensure the safety and security of visitors? What is our mission statement? How are we staying true to our values regarding the environment? How do we communicate these values to visitors?

Now ask the class to imagine that they work at the theme park. Use **still image** and **thought tracking** to create a living snapshot of the workers doing their different jobs. How are the workers identifiable? Should they have ID badges or security passes? Who checks them? Hone in on the security guards. Develop their backgrounds a little. What did they do before they became security guards? Do they like their jobs? What do they have to do each day at work? You could create **occupational mimes** of a day in the life of the guards with the children, in groups, showing different incidents that have taken place in the theme park. You could use the medium of still image if the acting threatens to get a little too boisterous.

Set up the classroom as the security office. What would be in there? You could use sticky notes to label the space. Sit the children down and explain that they have been called to the office as one of the guards has just discovered that, for the third night in a row, all the balls have been stolen from the ball pool in the toddlers' play area. Who could be responsible for this? Why on earth would someone steal from the toddlers' play area? Who could possibly need so many balls? Let the children chew over this news and compile questions about the situation. You can discuss these questions while sticking to the narrative direction of the session.

Next, introduce a CCTV image that has been found – this could be a sketch or a photograph, depending on what you can source. The image shows a man standing inside the ball pool, carrying a small dog in his arms.

The children are invited to compile further questions that they would like to ask the man in the image. Listen to and discuss the questions. When commenting on the questions, include nods back to the theme park context. For example, if a child wants to ask the man, "Why are you taking the balls away?" comment, "That's a good question, the balls belong in the theme park's ball pool, don't they?" Guide the children away from more general questions like "Where do you live?" or "What's your dog called?" This helps to stop the narrative from straying.

Get into role to answer the children's questions as the ball thief. Begin this by introducing yourself and your dog. Explain that you've been out of work for a long time. You used to work on a farm – the farm was actually right here where the theme park now stands – but you lost your job when the farmer sold the land. You used to think of the other farm workers as your family because you don't have any real family of your own. But they all lost their jobs too and now most of them have moved away. Your beloved dog, which was a working dog on the farm, is all the family you have left. Then answer the children's questions in a press conference style **hot seat**.

Once you have finished hot seating, explain why you committed your crime. Reveal that your dog is sick and that the vet recommended physiotherapy, saying that a bath of plastic balls would help to alleviate the animal's pain. After a botched attempt to bring the dog into the theme park, you decided to steal the balls to put in the bath at home.

Let the children decide what to do next …

Do the children feel some responsibility for the man and the dog? After all, they lost their livelihood and home when the theme park was built. What can they do to help? Are there any jobs that the man could do that would allow him to keep his dog with him? Could they explore if there are other people who were affected in such a way? What would happen if the theme park started hiring local people who were in some kind of difficulty? Who might they employ and why?

While one man and his dog might seem disconnected from the initial theme, one of the central ideas here is getting the children to think more ethically and widely and to consider the less likely consequences of actions. We're practising transference.

Stepping Stones

You could:

- Write some questions you would use in a job interview for a roller coaster operator and role play the responses.

- Consider the theme parks of the future. What might a theme park look like in 2118? Will we even need to leave our houses to visit them?

- Design the scariest or most thrilling ride you can think of. When does the search for the ultimate thrill end?

- Describe a seaside theme park that is closed for the winter. Imagine that your job is to look after it while it is closed for the season. What would you do? How would you feel? Would you rather work there in the summer? What might happen in the deserted park?

- Write an explanation of how forces impact on human experience of a ride.

- Think about what happens to your stomach when you go down a hill on a roller coaster. Find out if this is an emotional or physical response, or both. Explain it. You could do this as a piece of descriptive or scientific writing, a presentation, or any other method of your choosing.

- Visit a theme park.

The Bedrock – Relevance is Not Limiting

One of the key themes we're trying to explore in this book is the means by which we can bring the ordinary into focus and find the curriculum in familiar contexts. Most children are aware of theme parks even if they've not personally visited one. But it's not enough to simply select elements of the curriculum and make them familiar in order to make learning "relevant". If we only ever taught children what was relevant to them – i.e. within the frame of their existing experience – there would be little enrichment for many. The idea of relevance is itself complex. It is as much about making the unfamiliar and the difficult feel purposeful to children as it is about making the familiar more challenging. There is, or should be, a difficulty in relevance – a sense that all is not as it first seems, that it warrants further investigation. As such, we utilise curiosity in order to push children into needing and wanting to acquire knowledge.

Take, for example, the idea in the secondary landmarks section about creating a theme park with the express aim of making physics concepts understandable to visitors. In order to achieve this brief, the children need to be expressly taught the concepts – they need to understand them. They then need to work out how the concepts apply to common fairground rides. How is gravity utilised? How are forces used to give riders the thrills they seek? How are roller coasters pulled uphill? How do we control the speed on the downhills so that the carriages don't fall off the track? What happens when a ride loops the loop? Why doesn't the carriage fall off? How do we know it won't stop halfway round? These questions force the children to link their knowledge to a context but, more than that, they can then be charged with the responsibility of teaching others, through informative texts, what they know about how the rides are working. We have already discussed how being told that you will have to teach a concept or area of knowledge to someone else makes it more memorable. It is as if the brain is being primed for purpose, making what it then receives seem more important. As such, giving children tasks in which they are responsible for imparting and explaining knowledge to others (even if these others are fictional), is one way of helping to make learning more memorable and meaningful.[1] Especially if you can then also factor in risk and responsibility. What if their knowledge of physics is inaccurate? What if one of the rides failed?

As is the case throughout this book, we're working at the interface of imagination, ethical integrity and knowledge. Bringing these three aspects of human endeavour together helps children to see that, in order to have a positive influence in the world, they need to be not only knowledgeable but able to apply knowledge at points of dilemma where there are no black and white answers. This is how we elevate learning beyond the *what* to the *what if* and *what might be possible.* And to do this, we couple relevance and imagination.

The great German playwright Bertolt Brecht, desperate to find a theatrical means by which his audience might be inspired to "change the world", developed a system of disruption in his plays in which the familiar became unfamiliar – in which the audience were jostled out of passivity into deeper modes of thinking. He called this the *Verfremdungseffekt* – the alienation or distancing effect. Modern day cognitive scientists would probably regard this effect as a form of "cognitive disequilibrium", a concept we have discussed previously.[2]

Relevance is too comfortable for learners if it is not coupled with the unexpected, but that's not a reason to ignore it altogether. Finding contexts for learning with which children will connect does matter – the theme park here is not a frivolous choice which betrays low expectation. It is a way into much deeper and, actually, much darker thinking. Responsibility, safety, the unknown – these are important aspects of learning and need to be explored. Many of our young people come undone in familiar settings – reacting against the routine by pushing boundaries, taking risks and underestimating danger – we only have to see the number of accidents that take place on railway lines to see how devastating the consequences of this can be. So make sure to introduce them to the unfamiliar. Break the complacency and find the difficulty in the everyday.

....

1   Brown et al., *Make It Stick.*
2   D'Mello and Graesser, Dynamics of affective states.

The END OF THE BEGINNING

The prickly matter of assessment ...

But how do you evidence it?

None of these chapters offer an assessment scheme or set of success criteria, but every single one offers rich contexts in which to carry out all kinds of assessment tasks. There are mathematical calculations to be done and conversations to be had. There are reams to be written and knowledge to be gathered, considered and used. All of these tasks offer opportunities for assessment and your existing assessment criteria can be mapped onto them. These contexts are about making children *want* to write and *want* to calculate – helping them see value in their learning and remember *what* they did and *why*.

But it might help to bear these points in mind as you consider how to evidence this learning:

- Remember that in the UK accountability system, as in most international settings, inspectors are clear that they don't expect to see evidence of spoken tasks and oral feedback in books. They do expect to hear from the children themselves and to see from their work that they are in receipt of a stimulating, effective education and that they can articulate their learning. You could get children to write accounts and evaluations of what they've done, but don't do this for the inspectors – do it because reflective evaluation is good practice.

- You can use your walls to record key vocabulary, learning points, ideas and pieces of information. We call these wonder walls – they become a timeline of learning and can be photographed, added to and discussed.

- The clarity of your explanations and questions is key to this way of working. In many contexts, children are expected to heighten their language and stretch their vocabulary. Don't dumb down your language – instead, when you use complex vocabulary, offer an explanation or synonym to strengthen understanding. Encourage children to incorporate their heightened language when they speak and write.

◉ All the ideas here are underpinned by opportunities for the children to access and create texts. Find model texts so they can see plenty of examples of the forms they are being asked to write – be they storybooks, information leaflets, newspaper reports, websites and so on. All the contexts should be text rich and offer lots of opportunities to read, analyse and write.

◉ There are numeracy opportunities woven throughout the ideas for you to exploit – from creating timelines, to working out the ages of trees, to costing up materials, to mapping out locations. This is not to say that you don't need to teach knowledge and skills explicitly, but that there are many opportunities to practise what the children have learned. See these exercises as a test – but an exciting test!

No conclusion

So there you have it. Ten places to go, ten worlds to explore and many more than ten potential projects that will shake your children's imaginations – giving them the experience and opportunity to really think about the world out there without having to leave the classroom. We hope that what you have read has also shaken your own imagination and enabled you to see how to wrap what might otherwise be mundane curriculum coverage inside compelling contexts and ideas that really matter. Take the ideas and make them your own. Share them with your children and begin the exciting task of charting the unknown. And, above all, be optimistic, for in the words of Helen Keller:

"No pessimist ever discovered the secret of the stars or sailed to an uncharted land."

useful drama techniques

Throughout the book we've used key drama techniques in our stopover sections and these are explained more fully here. We've also added a few others that you might want to try as you develop the work. These techniques are *anchors* that can support thinking. Don't see them as prescriptive, just ideas that might help. We've used these strategies with the youngest of children and the most experienced of adults to stimulate thinking, expand the imagination and get learning up on its feet. Enjoy!

Collective role

This involves the children taking on the role of one character as a group and speaking different thoughts as that character. You might do this to show the confusion or complexity of an idea or dilemma as the character grapples with difficulty.

Conscience alley

When a character has a difficult decision to make, the children can form a tunnel for the character to walk through and offer them advice as they go. This could be used in any dilemma-led context.

Forum theatre

When developing a scene with children, you can sit the rest of the class around the group doing the acting, as "spectactors" rather than spectators. They can tip – by freezing the action and offering advice to the actors – or tag – by taking an actor's place. This makes the process of watching a story unfold more interactive, brings in new ideas and means all the children have the opportunity to participate.

Hot seating

This is when a character is interviewed or questioned. The teacher can assume the role of the character and be hot seated by the class, or the children can be primed to act as characters and interviewers. Always give the children time to prepare their role and their questions. However, the character may not be telling the truth so you can layer this by casting a "truth spell", meaning they have to answer honestly after giving their original answers. This might work well for the owner of the zoo who may not really have the animals' welfare at heart.

If the walls could talk

We made this name up because we weren't sure what this approach is formally called, but basically, if you have a character in a room – or any enclosed space, it could be a cage, container or crate – you sit four children around the character, facing outwards towards the class. Give each of them a statement about something that the "wall" has witnessed. The walls speak without emotion, only stating facts.

Mapping

Simples. Make the outline of your location on the floor using masking tape. Examples could include the floor plan of the castle or a cross section of the cave. Get the children to mark out key areas. This can also be done by drawing on a large sheet of paper with marker pens. Mapping acts as a reminder of scale, and stimulates the imagination. Alternatively, you could create your map from several large sheets of paper, writing a coordinate (A1, B2, C3, etc.) in the corner of each sheet. Once the whole group has mapped out the location, pairs of children can each take a sheet to focus on. They could write up a description of their location or a story about an event that took place there. Using the coordinates means you can easily see how the pieces of the map fit back together for subsequent discussion or whole group work.

Occupational mime

In silence and slowly, children mime a repeated action that represents a job they do.

Overheard conversation

Traditionally, this would be the teacher having a one-sided telephone conversation in front of the class to develop a story or build a point of tension. Now technology means this could be delivered as a text message, email, pre-recorded video message, etc. It's a way of seeding new information into a situation.

Role on the wall

This begins with the outline of a figure drawn on a sheet of paper – we like to style ours as a gingerbread person. When the children are exploring a character, they write down the information they discover about them inside the outline. These "facts" might include descriptions of their appearance, attitudes, values and behaviour. Around the figure they can write any questions or opinions they have. This might be a useful method of exploring any characters you encounter in the scenarios or, indeed, in any book.

Still image

This is when the children create a freeze frame depicting a moment in time within the context. This is also known as *tableau*. We can use still image to capture characters' reactions and to act out key moments within a story – for example, the villagers deciding what to do when they are asked to wreck the ship.

Tableau vivant

Literally meaning "living picture", this is when the children act out key moments, but by moving slowly from one still image to another (and perhaps back again). It can be used to create contrasts – for example, switching between different characters' points of view. You could use this technique to mark key moments in almost any of the scenarios.

Teacher in role

By speaking *as* someone else, the teacher can share key points within the context with virtually no preparation time. Not to be seen as acting – in the sense that you can just speak the lines without having to fully assume character and deliver an Oscar-worthy performance – it's a strategy that can deliver information to move learning and thinking on. This is useful for hearing about first-hand experiences or delivering news or instructions.

Thought tracking

This is when the children, often in role as a character, are asked to report what they are thinking. Thought tracking is frequently used alongside still image to explore characters' reactions and thoughts, in addition to their actions – for example, when we see the theme park employees at work. The children can speak their thoughts, or use whiteboards or paper as thought bubbles.

BIBLIOGRAPHY

USEFUL BOOKS AND POEMS FOR IN THE CLASSROOM

The Forest

Into the Forest – Anthony Browne

The Gruffalo – Julia Donaldson and Axel Scheffler

The Lorax – Dr. Seuss

The Castle

"Christabel" – Samuel Taylor Coleridge

George and the Dragon – Christopher Wormell

Over at the Castle – Boni Ashburn and Kelly Murphy

"Stopping by Woods on a Snowy Evening" and "The Road Not Taken" – Robert Frost

The Princess Bride – William Goldman

The Graveyard

Badger's Parting Gifts – Susan Varley

Michael Rosen's Sad Book – Michael Rosen and Quentin Blake

Neverwhere – Neil Gaiman

The Graveyard Book – Neil Gaiman

The Mountain

Geographics: Mountains – Izzi Howell

Island on Fire – Alexandra Witze and Jeff Kanipe

The Hobbit – J. R. R. Tolkien

Touching the Void – Joe Simpson

The Ship

Journey to the River Sea – Eva Ibbotson

Kensuke's Kingdom – Michael Morpurgo

Kidnapped – Robert Louis Stevenson

Life of Pi – Yann Martel

Lost and Found – Oliver Jeffers

Moonfleet – John Meade Falkner

The Lighthouse Keeper series – Ronda Armitage and David Armitage

"The Rime of the Ancient Mariner" – Samuel Taylor Coleridge

The Universe

How to Build a Universe – Brian Cox and Robin Ince

How to Catch a Star – Oliver Jeffers

Man on the Moon – Simon Bartram

The Darkest Dark – Chris Hadfield and the Fan Brothers

The Way Back Home – Oliver Jeffers

The Wasteland

Rotten Island – William Steig

Survival Camp – Bear Grylls

The Martian – Andy Weir

The Waste Land – T. S. Eliot

Uno's Garden – Graeme Base

The Zoo

Dear Zoo – Rod Campbell

Suddenly! – Colin McNaughton

The Arrival – Shaun Tan

The Tiger Who Came to Tea – Judith Kerr

The Zookeeper's Wife – Diane Ackerman

Zoo – Anthony Browne

The Cave

"Endymion" – John Keats

The Odyssey – Homer

The Weirdstone of Brisingamen – Alan Garner

Ug: Boy Genius of the Stone Age – Raymond Briggs

The Theme Park

Fair's Fair – Leon Garfield

Fairground Lights – Fran Nuño and Enrique Quevedo

The Night Circus – Erin Morgenstern

Wonder Show – Hannah Barnaby

FURTHER READING FOR TEACHERS

Abraham, A. (2016) The imaginative mind, *Human Brain Mapping*, 37(11): 4197–4211.

Anderson, P. and Jané-Llopis, E. (2011) Mental health and global well-being, *Health Promotion International*, 26(1): 147–155. Available at: https://academic.oup.com/heapro/article/26/suppl_1/i147/686692/Mental-health-and-global-well-being.

Arya, D. J. and Maul, A. (2012) The role of the scientific discovery narrative in middle school science education: an experimental study, *Journal of Educational Psychology*, 104(4): 1022–1032.

Baddeley, A. D. and Hitch, G. (1974) Working memory. In G. H. Bower (Ed.), *The Psychology of Learning and Motivation: Advances in Research and Theory*, Vol. 8. New York: Academic Press, pp. 47–89.

Bateson, P. and Martin, P. (2013) *Play, Playfulness, Creativity and Innovation*. Cambridge: Cambridge University Press.

Bergland, C. (2013) Cortisol: Why "the stress hormone" is public enemy no. 1, *Psychology Today* (23 January). Available at: https://www.psychologytoday.com/blog/the-athletes-way/201301/cortisol-why-the-stress-hormone-is-public-enemy-no-1.

Bergland, C. (2013) The Neuroscience of Empathy, *Psychology Today* (10 October). Available at: https://www.psychologytoday.com/blog/the-athletes-way/201310/the-neuroscience-empathy.

Berk, L. S., Tan, S. A., Fry, W. F., Napier, B. J., Lee, J. W., Hubbard, R. W., Lewis, J. E. and Eby, W. C. (1989) Neuroendocrine and stress hormone changes during mirthful laughter, *The American Journal of the Medical Sciences*, 298(6): 390–396. Available at: https://doi.org/10.1097/00000441-198912000-00006.

Biesta, G. (2013) *The Beautiful Risk of Education*. Boulder, CO: Paradigm.

Blakemore, S-J. (2012) The mysterious workings of the teenage brain, *Ted.com* [video]. Available at: https://www.ted.com/talks/sarah_jayne_blakemore_the_mysterious_workings_of_the_adolescent_brain.

Brown, P. C., Roediger, H. L. and McDaniel, M. A. (2014) *Make It Stick: The Science of Successful Learning*. Cambridge, MA: Belknap Press.

Bruner, J. (1976) *The Process of Education*. Cambridge, MA: Harvard University Press.

Claxton, G. (2016) *Intelligence in the Flesh: Why Your Mind Needs Your Body Much More Than It Thinks*. New Haven, CT: Yale University Press.

Curran, A. (2008) *The Little Book of Big Stuff About the Brain: The True Story of Your Amazing Brain.* Carmarthen: Independent Thinking Press.

Damasio, A. (1995) *Descartes' Error: Emotion, Reason and the Human Brain.* New York: Putnam.

Daughters, S., Gorka, S., Matusiewicz, A. and Anderson, K. (2013) Gender specific effect of psychological stress and cortisol reactivity on adolescent risk taking, *Journal of Abnormal Child Psychology*, 41(5): 749–758. doi:10.1007/s10802-013-9713-4

Dee, T. S. and Sievertsen, H. H. (2015) *The Gift of Time? School Starting Age and Mental Health*, NBER Working Paper No. 21610. Cambridge, MA: The National Bureau of Economic Research. Available at: http://www.nber.org/papers/w21610.

Demir, Ö. E., Levine, S. C. and Goldin-Meadow, S. (2014) A tale of two hands: children's early gesture use in narrative production predicts later narrative structure in speech, *Journal of Child Language*, 42: 662–681. doi:10.1017/S0305000914000415

D'Mello, S. and Graesser, A. (2012) Dynamics of affective states during complex learning, *Learning and Instruction*, 22(2): 145–157.

Feynman, R. (1956) The Relation of Science and Religion, transcript of a talk given by Dr. Feynman at the Caltech YMCA Lunch Forum on 2 May 1956. Available at: http://calteches. library.caltech.edu/49/2/Religion.htm.

Goldin-Meadow, S. and Wagner, S. M. (2005) How our hands help us learn, *Trends in Cognitive Sciences*, 9(5): 234–241. doi:10.1016/j.tics.2005.03.006

Greenfield, S. (2011) *You and Me: The Neuroscience of Identity.* London: Notting Hill Editions.

Howard-Jones, P. (2008) *Fostering Creative Thinking: Co-constructed Insights from Neuroscience and Education.* Bristol: Higher Education Academy, Education Subject Centre.

Huang, E. (2017) A spate of student suicides is forcing Hong Kong to confront its cutthroat school system, *Quartz* (13 February). Available at: https://qz.com/904483/a-spate-of-student-suicides-is-forcing-hong-kong-to-confront-its-cutthroat-school-system/.

Itkowitz, C. (2016) Harvard researchers discovered the one thing everyone needs for happier, healthier lives, *The Washington Post* (2 March). Available at: https://www.washingtonpost.com/news/inspired-life/wp/2016/03/02/harvard-researchers-discovered-the-one-thing-everyone-needs-for-happier-healthier-lives/?utm_term=.3c67606bc699.

Jaccard, J. and Jacoby, J. (2010) *Theory Construction and Model-Building Skills: A Practical Guide for Social Scientists.* New York: Guilford Press.

Jay, T., Willis, B., Thomas, P., Taylor, R., Moore, N., Burnett, C., Merchant, G. and Stevens, A. (2017) *Dialogic Teaching: Evaluation Report and Executive Summary.* London: Education Endowment Foundation. Available at: https://educationendowmentfoundation.org.uk/public/files/Projects/Evaluation_Reports/Dialogic_Teaching_Evaluation_Report.pdf.

Kaufman, S. (2013) The real neuroscience of creativity, *Scientific American* (19 August). Available at: https://blogs.scientificamerican.com/beautiful-minds/the-real-neuroscience-of-creativity/.

MacKenzie, S. (2016) Professor Brian Cox: education is as important to security as missile defence, *The Big Issue* (28 November). Available at: https://www.bigissue.com/interviews/professor-brian-cox-education-important-security-missile-defence/.

Mercer, N. (2000) *Words and Minds: How We Use Language to Think Together.* Abingdon: Routledge.

Michaels, S., O'Connor, C. and Resnick, L. (2008) Deliberative discourse idealized and realized: accountable talk in the classroom and in civic life, *Studies in Philosophy and Education*, 27(4): 283–297.

Myatt, M. (2016) *Hopeful Schools: Building Humane Communities.* Mary Myatt Learning Limited.

National Advisory Committee on Creative and Cultural Education (1999) *All Our Futures: Creativity, Culture and Education*. Available at: http://sirkenrobinson.com/pdf/allourfutures.pdf.

OECD (2017) *United Kingdom: Country Note – Results from PISA 2015 (Volume III): Students' Well-Being*. Available at: http://www.oecd.org/pisa/PISA2015-students-well-being-United-Kingdom.pdf.

Pink, D. (2009) *Drive: The Surprising Truth About What Motivates Us*. New York: Riverhead.

Sagan, C. (1994) *Pale Blue Dot: A Vision of the Human Future in Space*. New York: Random House.

Schellenberg, G. E. (2004) Music lessons enhance IQ, *Psychological Science*, 15(8): 511–514. Available at: https://doi.org/10.1111/j.0956-7976.2004.00711.x.

Singer, T. (2015) How to build a caring economy, *World Economic Forum* (24 January). Available at: https://www.weforum.org/agenda/2015/01/how-to-build-a-caring-economy/.

Smith, M. (2018) *The Emotional Learner: Understanding Emotions, Learners and Achievement*. Abingdon: Routledge.

Stossel, S. (2013) What makes us happy, revisited, *The Atlantic* (May). Available at: https://www.theatlantic.com/magazine/archive/2013/05/thanks-mom/309287/.

Ward, H. (2017) UK pupils among the world's unhappiest, *tes* (19 April). Available at: https://www.tes.com/news/school-news/breaking-news/uk-pupils-among-worlds-unhappiest.

Willingham, D. (2004) Ask the cognitive scientist: the privileged status of story, *American Educator*. Available at: http://www.aft.org/periodical/american-educator/summer-2004/ask-cognitive-scientist.

Wolf, O. (2009) Stress and memory in humans: twelve years of progress? *Brain Research*, 1293: 142–154. Available at: https://doi.org/10.1016/j.brainres.2009.04.013.